WISEBLOOD ESSAYS IN CONTEMPORARY CULTURE NO. 19

NO ONE WAS PAYING ANY ATTENTION TO THE SKY

Flannery O'Connor and Modernity

Fr. Damian Ference

with a Foreword by
Christopher Scalia

Wiseblood Books
2025

Copyright © 2025 Wiseblood Books

All rights reserved, including the right to reproduce this book or any portions thereof in any form whatsoever except for brief quotations in book reviews. For information, address the publisher:

>WISEBLOOD BOOKS
>*Joshua Hren, Editor-in-Chief*
>Post Office Box 870
>Menomonee Falls, WI 53052
>www.wisebloodbooks.com

ISBN: 978-1-951319-06-9

*For Brittney B,
and to all those fighting the good fight.*

Take Up and Read
By Christopher J. Scalia

One of my favorite moments in Flannery O'Connor's fiction occurs at the end of "Good Country People," a short story first published in 1955. The central character, an arrogant intellectual christened Joy (but who tellingly prefers to go by Hulga) has just been conned by a man she had thought was a good Christian and an uneducated country bumpkin—in short, her inferior. The last we see of Hulga, she is peering out of a barn, her vision impaired, the con man's "blue figure struggling successfully over [a] green speckled lake." That is, he seems to be walking on water.

We know better: with Hulga's sight compromised, the grass only looks like a lake. But the imagery signals that this unworthy man has performed a minor miracle by curing Hulga, healing her spiritual blindness. He may not be Christlike, but a hopeful reading of the story infers that his role in her redemption is. Humbled, Hulga has the opportunity to be redeemed, to abandon the cynicism and joylessness with which she views the world.

O'Connor excelled at these stark and often shocking scenes of ambiguous and ironic redemption. Such epiphanic moments like this are one reason O'Connor's fiction remains so popular among Christians (Catholics in particular) and non-Christians alike. Catholics have a special admiration for her ability to convey her deep and abiding Catholic faith in a way that is both rooted in tradition and unmistakably modern, orthodox without being didactic.

O'Connor's stories teem with characters like Hulga, characters who—as Father Damian Ference puts it in these pages—"embod[y]. . . modern, rational, highly educated scientism or skepticism." There is an element of self-criticism to these characters. It's hard to miss the overlap between O'Connor and Hulga, for example: artist and character alike were well-educated, disabled (O'Connor suffered from lupus and required crutches; Hulga has a wooden leg), and lived with their occasionally overbearing mothers. Both were deeply interested in philosophy. Hulga's philosophy, though, is atheistic and—as her change of name suggests—joyless.

O'Connor, on the other hand, rejected the philosophical moorings of her (and our) time. Instead, she embraced the philosophical teachings of St. Thomas Aquinas and immersed herself in the works of his twentieth-century expositors. Nobody is better at tracing her intellectual interests, and showing what she meant when she called herself a Hillbilly Thomist, than Father Damian Ference.

Father Ference's admiration for O'Connor is one of the first things I knew about him before we met in the early 2010s. My wife and I had befriended a young couple who had just moved to the Appalachian town we then called home, and Father Ference—F. D., as they affectionately called him—was an important figure in their lives. He had brought the young man into the Church, was preparing the couple for marriage, and would eventually celebrate their nuptial Mass. (I'm happy to report that F. D.'s sermon at the wedding was exceptional, and featured the combination of philosophical depth and casual charm that make his writing so worthwhile.)

One thing that impressed me about Father Ference even before I met him was that he had founded (and still runs) a summer institute for rising high school seniors called *Tolle Lege*. That name is a reference to St. Augustine's *Confessions*: Augustine heard a voice chanting the imperative, which means *take up and read*. The saint interpreted the calling as a command from the Almighty and promptly read Scripture. A great name for a summer institute! Topping it off, the program's logo at the time was a peacock feather: a tribute to O'Connor's love for that bird.

O'Connor was an apt symbol for Father Ference's institute because, as the volume you're holding now makes clear, she abided by the command to take up and read. Father Ference shows us O'Connor's library shelves, brings us into her rooms of study, discusses the letters she wrote her friends and the reviews she wrote for her diocesan paper, to reveal the artist's intellectual seriousness and respect for the Catholic philosophical tradition. Although she was not a philosopher, she understood that she could practice and understand her faith more fully—and practice the craft of fiction more powerfully—if she immersed herself in the greatest thought that the Church produced.

Today, many traditionally-minded Catholics perceive the pre-Vatican II Church as being free of saccharine fluff and airy thinking, full of intellectual rigor and serious devotion. O'Connor's concern regarding the excessively sentimental piety among many Catholics and within Catholic art suggests otherwise. She also recognized that the modern world was at odds with her belief. Yet, as Father Ference shows, she did not flee from modernity. Instead, she sought to convey the Thomistic thought she so admired in terms and modes that would resonate with her contemporaries. This, as Father Ference well understands, is a hallmark of the exceptional evangelist.

Father Ference (like O'Connor) excels at explaining complex ideas succinctly for non-specialists. You may not be familiar with some of the philosophers who shaped O'Connor's thinking, and whom Father Ference explores here; others—Aquinas, Descartes, Spinoza—will be more familiar. Regardless, you will come away from this work with a deeper understanding of the intellectual framework undergirding O'Connor's art and her protests against modernity. Ference's keen concluding analysis of her first novel, *Wise Blood*, makes clear that O'Connor's interest in philosophy was more than dilettantism: she melded it seamlessly into her creative vision. In the process, Fr. Ference can help us recognize these philosophical underpinnings when we read her other works—which this study will no doubt inspire many of us to do.

Flannery O'Connor and Modernity

"Her picture of the modern world is literally terrifying."[1] These are the words that literary critic Caroline Gordon used to describe Flannery O'Connor's first novel, *Wise Blood*, and they could easily extend to all of O'Connor's fiction as well as her letters, essays, lectures, journals, and even her cartoons. O'Connor considered herself a Hillbilly Thomist, which is to say that Thomistic epistemology and hillbilly common sense agree that knowledge begins with the senses. It is also to say that although O'Connor was an artist and not a trained philosopher, she was an intellectual wary of intellectualism and believed that true artists must be humble in the face of what-is.[2] For O'Connor, *what-is* was reality, as known by reason by way of the senses and broadened by faith. It is not an idealized or pixilated world, but the real world, where peacocks are peacocks, and eggs are eggs, and a woman is a woman. Flannery O'Connor targeted modernity as a philosophical movement that abandons God and rejects Christian faith, while, at the same time, prudently avoiding the temptation to isolate herself altogether from the modern world with its many propitious scientific advancements and practical conveniences.[3] Paul Elie notes, "She was an odd kind of believer, one situated in modernity but not formed by it, indeed formed in opposition to modernity and determined to maintain her independence from it through her religion."⁴ O'Connor sought in her own way to follow the biblical principle of being *in* the (modern) world without being *of* the (modern) world,⁵ and this mentality forms an essential attribute of her prophetic vision.

In her senior year at Georgia State College for Women (GSCW), O'Connor enrolled in an Introduction to Modern Philosophy course taught by Professor George Beiswanger, and her biographer Brad Gooch argues that this course was foundational to O'Connor's understanding and critique of modernity:

> Dr. Beiswanger's class was a survey of modern philosophers, the assigned textbook, *The Making of the Modern Mind*, by John Herman Randall, Jr. As Beiswanger has recalled, the book was "an academic best-seller whose viewpoint (and mine) was secular humanist (grounded in Pragmatism) and took for granted that the Renaissance and the Age of Enlightenment set the Western mind free from the benightedness of Medieval thought (from Thomas Aquinas, etc.)." The hero of the course was the seventeenth-century French philosopher Descartes, for relying in his *Discourse on Method* (1637) on mathematics and science to unlock the secrets of a purely material world. Yet a few weeks into the course, the professor became aware of a persistent, subtle scowl: "Flannery sat in class, listened intently, took notes, and without her saying a word, it became

clear that she didn't believe a word of what I was saying."⁶

Flannery O'Connor was exceptionally well-read, so it would be difficult if not impossible to cite every source that informed her critique of modernity; however, Romano Guardini and Étienne Gilson are certainly two of O'Connor's most important philosophical influences in this regard. She read many of their works, wrote reviews of their books, and we know from her correspondence that she generously referenced their thoughts and recommended their writings to friends and colleagues. I spent significant time with O'Connor's personal library in the Special Collections at Georgia College and State University researching this book, specifically noting O'Connor's underlining and marginal annotations in the books cited below.

The first and second parts of this essay, then, will show the philosophical influence of Guardini and Gilson on the art of Flannery O'Connor. The third part will look to four major philosophical themes of modernity presented in the works of Guardini and Gilson that are key to understanding Flannery O'Connor's art and her Hillbilly Thomism: *the self as the center of existence; the disregard for mystery; a general distrust of the concrete;* and *the subordination of reason.* Finally, in the fourth and final section of this essay, we will show how these four philosophical themes are revealed and addressed by O'Connor in her first novel, *Wise Blood*.

Romano Guardini

That Flannery O'Connor, the self-professed Hillbilly Thomist, would be drawn to and influenced by the writings of Romano Guardini (1885–1968) comes as something of a surprise, for Guardini made a name for himself in part by writing against the Thomists of his day. Born in 1885 and educated in the finest schools in Germany,[7] Guardini attempted in his scholarship to navigate the choppy intellectual waters of the early twentieth century. Holger Zaborowski explains:

> The years after 1918 were culturally and intellectually perhaps the most vivid years of recent German history—full of tensions, ruptures, and contradictions. The reasons for this are as simple as complex. It was clear that it was no longer possible simply to follow the modern trajectory of the eighteenth and nineteenth centuries. The narratives of the Enlightenment tradition, of progress, reason, science, and freedom became deeply questionable.... New points of reference and of meaning became important—among many others Nietzsche, the radical critic of the Western tradition, rather than Hegel, who claimed to complete this very tradition; Kierkegaard, the fideist, rather than Kant, the rationalist; St. Paul, read as a radical decisionist, rather than the liberal theologians of the nineteenth century; Augustine, the early Christian existentialist, rather than Aquinas, the systematic thinker.[8]

Guardini, who was not only a philosopher and theologian but also a Catholic priest, was concerned on one hand with the "rampant agnosticism and atheism"[9] of his day, yet on the other hand "he regarded critically the specific kind of anti-modernism—provincial, anti-intellectual, and authoritarian—that was prevalent in early twentieth-century Catholicism."[10] Guardini sought to find a position that recognized the historical and concrete situation of his day[11] while adhering to the eternal and unchanging truths of his Christian faith. This position resulted in Guardini's rejection of Thomism, at least in regard to its initial engagement (or lack of engagement) with modernity,[12] and his embrace of an Augustinian existentialism, which "seemed to offer the possibility of a more fruitful engagement with the modern world," as his philosophical and theological starting point.[13]

Guardini's attraction to Augustine and his aversion to textbook Thomism (but not St. Thomas Aquinas) is understandable, for he found the Thomism of his day to be cold, overly rationalistic, and narrowly moralistic, leaving him in search of a philosophy that involved the whole human person, with special emphasis on the themes of freedom and love.[14] In Augustine Guardini discovered an unmatched exemplar of such a philosophy, reasoning in his introduction to *The Conversion of Augustine*:

> From the indivisible whole that is known as St. Augustine [this study] focuses its attention on that realm where philosophy and theology are not yet separated, as they are today, not even as widely

> separated as they were in the Middle Ages . . . a realm in which Christian existence was considered a unit from which thought emerged and to which it returned without ever bothering about methodical distinctions.[15]

The important Aristotelian-Thomistic principle, *that which is received is received according to the mode of the receiver*,[16] helps clarify Guardini's attraction to Augustine. Guardini harbored a deep suspicion of any philosophy that presented itself to him as overly rationalistic,[17] whether German Idealism or the Thomism of his day.[18] By contrast, he found that Augustine presented the same basic dogmatic truths of Christianity as did St. Thomas Aquinas,[19] but in a manner Guardini found to be less systematic, more existential,[20] and hence more credible to the age in which he lived.

O'Connor's Reading of Guardini

Flannery O'Connor first mentions Romano Guardini in a letter to Sally Fitzgerald dated December 26, 1954. She writes, "I am reading everything I can of Romano Guardini's [Italian priest and theologian]. Have you become acquainted with his work? A book called *The Lord* of his is very fine."[21] O'Connor specifically mentions *The Lord* five times and "Msgr. Guardini" a total of seventeen times in her published letters. She owned several books by Guardini[22] and reviewed six of them for her diocesan newspaper.[23] O'Connor eventually realized that Guardini was German[24] and noted that in addition to being a theologian he was also a "Professor of Philosophy at the University of Munich and was named House Chaplain to the Pope in 1952."[25]

O'Connor saw in Guardini a credible, intelligent guide who offered her an example of how to navigate the modern era as a serious Catholic. She writes:

> The first most noticeable characteristic of Monsignor Guardini's writing is the total absence of pious cliché. When he considers the doctrine or liturgy or practice of the Church, he rethinks these in the light of modern difficulties and preoccupations.... With Monsignor Guardini, one feels that these difficulties are his own, that he does not stand on a height above the modern mind coping with its own agonizing problems but infused with grace.[26]

O'Connor's references to "modern difficulties and preoccupations" and "the modern mind" are indicative of her constant lookout for ways to present her Catholic worldview to a modern reader. This is not to say that O'Connor ever abandoned her Hillbilly Thomism for Guardini's more Augustinian approach—we have no evidence that O'Connor had any knowledge of Guardini's trouble with the Thomists of his day, so it is safe to say she understood Guardini's philosophical and theological contributions as connatural with her instinctive respect for Thomism.[27] In a letter to Betty Hester dated September 24, 1955, O'Connor displayed her understanding of this non-competitive relation between Thomas Aquinas and Romano Guardini:

> I am learning to walk on crutches and I feel like a large stiff anthropoid ape who has no cause to be thinking of St. Thomas or Aristotle; however, you are making me more of a Thomist than I ever was before and an Aristotelian where I never was before. I am one, of course, who believes that man is created in the image and likeness of God. I believe that all creation is good but that what has free choice is more completely God's image than what does not have it; also I define humility differently from you. Msgr. Guardini can explain that. I think it is good to have these differences defined.[28]

O'Connor knew that truth is truth, whether articulated in the thirteenth century or the twentieth, but she directed Hester to Guardini rather than to Aquinas because Guardini's philosophical and theological project engaged directly with the problems of a modern age that Aquinas's teachings could at best only anticipate.

In another letter to Hester dated August 11, 1956, O'Connor writes, "If Msgr. Guardini is the Msgr. Sheen of Europe then that only says how far Europe is ahead of us on that score."[29] What O'Connor saw in Guardini was an evangelist with the appeal of Fulton Sheen but more intellectually rigorous; someone who knew the perennial philosophy, who knew the Catholic tradition, and who was able to bring these into conversation with modernity with clarity, conviction, and credibility, which was ultimately what O'Connor desired to do in her own narrative art. She found in Guardini an intellectual mentor who deepened her love of truth and whose style she sought to emulate: "He proceeds slowly and with a simplicity that reveals a depth of meaning to the reader who is likewise willing to be in no hurry."[30]

Perhaps O'Connor's most important observation in regard to the writings of Guardini is in her review of *Practice in Prayer*, when she states, "His concerns are very much for the problems of modern man, in whom faith is often no more than a possibility. It is, in part, the realization of the modern condition that makes all of Monsignor Guardini's work so vital."[31] We see the same realization at work in O'Connor's description of her own readers: "My audience are the people who think God is dead. At least these are the people I am conscious of writing for."[32] O'Connor viewed Guardini as a model for navigating the rough waters of modernity as a believing Christian, and, likely without any knowledge of Guardini's conflicts with the Thomists of his day, she looked to him as a source of strength in the development of her own distinctive literary expression of Hillbilly Thomism.

Guardini's Influence on O'Connor

Romano Guardini influenced Flannery O'Connor's understanding of and response to modernity in two very important ways. Firstly, Guardini's writings were forever responding to what he understood to be the preeminent philosophical problem of modernity, *the alienation of man*.[33] Having rejected the pre-modern understanding of what Charles Taylor calls *the enchanted world*—wherein the order of the natural world bespeaks divine creation and God is implicated in the very existence of society[34]—modern man experiences alienation from God, the world, other people, and even, at times, himself. Guardini was so drawn to Augustine (and his *Confessions* in particular), because he found that Augustine understood alienation firsthand and offered a path forward toward integration. For Augustine, this alienation of man is ultimately a result of original sin, which turns man away from God and the world and turns him in on himself.[35] O'Connor owned and reviewed Guardini's *The Conversion of Augustine* and it is clear that this book made an impression upon her. In O'Connor's personal copy, she made a check mark next to this sentence: "We see him [Augustine] gradually being led by encounter and inner development, by experience, thought, and act, until at last the hour of ultimate decision is there, by which the inner and the outer man, conscience and way of life, exhortation and active being meet in complete accord."[36] O'Connor, like Guardini, found in Augustine an adequate response to the modern problem of man's alienation, and we will demonstrate in the following sections how that response made its way into her narrative art. Secondly, Guardini's pointed criticisms of inadequate responses to modernity, specifically by those within the Church, had a tremendous influence on O'Connor's narrative art, and it is to these criticisms we now turn.

Influenced by Guardini, O'Connor was highly suspicious of any literature, devotions, piety, or religious practices that made the Catholic faith appear to be unreasonable, anti-intellectual, or superstitious. In her review of *Meditations Before Mass* O'Connor quotes Guardini:

> Monsignor Guardini points out, "piety is inclined to neglect [Truth]... Not that it shuns or shies away from it, but it is remarkable how readily piety slides off into fantasy, sentimentality and exaggeration. Legends and devotional books offer only too frequent and devastating proof of this; unfortunately piety is inclined to lose itself in the subjective, to become musty, turgid, unspiritual. Divine reality is never any of these..."[37]

As a Hillbilly Thomist, O'Connor was not interested in fantasy, sentimentality, or exaggeration,[38] but in realism, truth, and mystery. She followed Guardini's lead in cautioning others of the dangers present within her own Catholic tradition in the twentieth century. We see Guardini's strong influence on O'Connor in her letter to her friend John Lynch dated February 19, 1956:

> The *Ave Maria*[39] I have never seen but can only too well imagine. Of course this vapid Catholicism can't influence you except to want to be shut of it. The Catholic influence has to come at a deeper level. I was brought up in the novena-rosary tradition too, but you have to save yourself from it someway or dry up. I was struck in *All Manner of Men* with how limited the range of experience was—all those baby stories and nun stories and young girl stories—a nice vapid-

> Catholic distrust of finding God in action of any range and depth. This is not the kind of Catholicism that has saved me so many years of learning to write, but then this is not Catholicism at all...[40]

O'Connor—a prayerful woman with deep devotion to the Blessed Virgin Mary[41]—was not out to attack the devotional life, but to clarify that devotion and piety are no substitute for a rigorous intellectual life; indeed, true devotion and piety should lead to a love of truth, which demands an intellectual honesty often ignored by what she refers to as "vapid Catholicism."

In her review of Guardini's *Prayer in Practice*, O'Connor writes, "he makes it clear that many of the prayers found in current prayer books are not only useless to the development of the life of prayer, but positively harmful."[42] Guardini was concerned that the devotional literature of his day lacked truthfulness and a sense of honor,[43] a criticism that resonated with O'Connor. In the spirit of Guardini, O'Connor instructs Cecil Dawkins, "The only places you can really avoid the Pious Style are in the liturgy and in the Bible; and these are the places where the Church herself speaks..."[44] Guardini was an active player in the liturgical movement of the twentieth century, and he "presented the experience of the liturgy as an antidote to the cold rationalism and narrow moralism that he saw afflicting the Church of his day."[45] He was constantly directing his readers 'back to the sources' of the liturgy and the Bible as the solid theological ground on which to stand. As Joseph Ratzinger notes, "Guardini recognized that the liturgy is the true, *living* environment for the Bible and that the Bible can be properly understood only in this living context within which it first emerged."[46] Philosophically speaking, Guardini was concerned with first principles, and instructed his readers, including O'Connor, that returning to the first principles of liturgy and scripture was key to living in the modern world as a Catholic Christian.

Returning to the foundational sources or first principles of the Christian faith is a philosophical move that is vital to O'Connor's art, which is the reason she abhored pious cliché and was vigilant about her influences. She admits to Betty Hester, "I try militantly never to be affected by the pious language of the faithful but it is always coming out when you least expect it. In contrast to the pious language of the faithful, the liturgy is beautifully flat."[47] We note that O'Connor's concerns here regarding pious language stem from a distrust of sentimentality, which she understood as a threat to *what-is*, and therefore a real threat to her art. She informs Janet McKane, "I really dislike books of piety most of all. They do nothing for me and they corrupt most people's ear if nothing else"[48] It is very difficult to imagine O'Connor saying such things without the influence of Romano Guardini, who convinced her that to live in the modern world as a Catholic, one must be grounded in the depth of a reality that is not bound by time and space but which must be constantly re-discovered and re-presented in every time and space.

ÉTIENNE GILSON

Whereas O'Connor's admiration of Guardini may be surprising at first glance, the influence of Étienne Gilson, one of the leading voices in the Thomistic revival of the twentieth century, could hardly be more fitting.[49] Inspired by *Aeterni Patris*, Gilson's life mission was the study of the history of philosophy with special emphasis on the contribution of St. Thomas Aquinas. Gilson summarizes his foundational thesis here:

> In Thomism alone we have a system in which philosophic conclusions are deduced from purely rational premises. Theology remains in its proper place, that is to say at the head of the hierarchy of the sciences; based on divine revelation, from which it receives its principles, it constitutes a distinct science starting from faith and turning to reason only to draw out the content of faith or to protect it from error. Philosophy, doubtless, is subordinate to theology, but, as philosophy, it depends on nothing but its own proper method; based on human reason, owing all its truth to the self-evidence of its principles and the accuracy of its deductions, it reaches an accord with faith spontaneously and without having to deviate in any way from its own proper path. If it does so it is simply because it is true, and because one truth cannot contradict another.[50]

Although some controversy remains within Thomistic circles over Gilson's interpretation of Thomas and his argument for a *Christian philosophy*,[51] such in-house arguments were of no concern to Flannery O'Connor the narrative artist, as she understood Gilson as a major authority on philosophy in general, and on Thomism and aesthetics in particular.

Unlike Guardini, who was more Augustinian than Thomist (and yet still managed to positively influence O'Connor's Hillbilly Thomism), Gilson was a major player in the rehabilitation of Thomism's reputation in the twentieth century and wrote and lectured prolifically on medieval philosophy and the philosophy of St. Thomas Aquinas in particular. He confidently notes, "Personally, I do not say of Thomas that he was right, but that he *is* right. This has not been a preconceived principle guiding my historical study of Thomas Aquinas; it is its conclusion. But only those who have chosen Thomas as their guide know how it is possible to prefer him without despising the rest."[52] Gilson's interpretation of Thomas was very attractive to Flannery O'Connor and continues to attract an impressive readership within philosophical and theological circles today. In fact, outside of O'Connor's reading of Thomas himself and perhaps the works of Jacques Maritain, it is difficult to identify any author from whom O'Connor learned more about St. Thomas Aquinas and Thomism.

O'Connor's Reading of Gilson

We find two books written by Gilson in O'Connor's personal library, *The Unity of Philosophical Experience* and

Reason and Revelation in the Middle Ages; one book for which Gilson wrote the introduction, *An Essay in Aid of a Grammar of Assent* by John Henry Newman; and we know from letters to Betty Hester that O'Connor read at least two other books by Gilson.[53] O'Connor wrote reviews of Gilson's *Painting and Reality* and *Reason and Revelation in the Middle Ages*; she never published the latter review but it can be found in *The Presence of Grace*. O'Connor mentions Gilson six times in *The Habit of Being* and always in a most favorable tone. It is to these sources we now turn.

O'Connor's first mention of Étienne Gilson is found in a letter to Betty Hester: "Gilson is a vigorous writer, more than Maritain; the other thing I have read of his is *The Unity of Philosophical Experience*, which I am an admirer of."[54] *The Unity of Philosophical Experience* is a collection of lectures Gilson gave in 1936 at Harvard University in celebration of the 300th anniversary of the school's founding.[55] It is by no means an easy read, especially for someone like O'Connor with minimal formal training in philosophy, but there can be little doubt that O'Connor's knowledge of modern philosophy and its effects were influenced by this work. In his foreword Desmond FitzGerald explains Gilson's thesis:

> Gilson is not writing a history of philosophy but using the resources of the history of philosophy to study different intellectual experiments philosophers have undertaken. And the lesson Gilson infers from his study is that there has been a continual temptation across the centuries for brilliant thinkers to make

a similar mistake, namely, to attempt to reform the philosophy of their time according to the method and structure of another science.

To label these misadventures, Gilson coins new names: the theologism of Bonaventure, the psychologism of William of Ockham, the mathematicism of Descartes, the physicalism of Kant, and the sociologism of Comte. Gilson shows in a profound and witty way how the best intentions of these philosophers have ultimately resulted in skepticism, a loss of confidence in our ability to achieve philosophical truth. But Gilson was not despairing, for he was confident that philosophers who respected the nature of philosophy and the need for it to follow its own method could succeed. His aphorism here was: "Philosophy always buries its own undertakers."[56]

On almost every page of *The Unity of Philosophical Experience* Gilson argues that traditional metaphysics is the grounding of every science precisely because metaphysics is the first science, and that any time even the most brilliant thinker attempts to replace metaphysics with another science, that project ultimately fails, because no other science is equipped to replace the science of being. In the final chapter, Gilson presents a correction to a common philosophical pitfall of modernity when he writes, "Man is not a mind that thinks, but a being who knows other beings as true, who loves them as good, and who enjoys them as beautiful."[57] This line of thinking had great influence on O'Connor's understanding of modernity and presents itself repeatedly in her art.[58]

It is worth noting that when O'Connor wrote to friends and colleagues who were struggling with understanding some philosophical issue, particularly in light of Christian faith and modernity, she was quick to recommend the work of Gilson. For example, to Cecil Dawkins she writes, "Anyway, to discover the Church you have to set out by yourself. The French Catholic novelists were a help to me in this—Bloy, Bernanos, Mauriac. In philosophy, Gilson, Maritain and Gabriel Marcel, an Existentialist,"[59] and to Alfred Corn she writes, "Don't think that you have to abandon reason to be a Christian. A book that might help you is *The Unity of Philosophical Experience* by Étienne Gilson."[60]

Although O'Connor never reviewed *The Unity of Philosophical Experience* for her diocesan newspaper, interestingly, she does mention the work in her unpublished review of Gilson's *Reason and Revelation in the Middle Ages*. She concludes the review with these two sentences: "These lectures are an excellent introduction to Gilson's *The Unity of Philosophical Experience*, a book indispensable to an understanding of the modern age. In addition to the intellectual value of anything written by Gilson, it is always a pleasure to read him for the vigor and lucidity of his style."[61] We will see some very clear examples in the following sections of how truly indispensable this book is to O'Connor's understanding of the modern age.

Painting and Reality is a collection of the A. W. Mellon Lectures in the Fine Arts that Gilson delivered at the National Gallery of Art in Washington, D.C. in 1955. O'Connor's personal copy is absent from her library archive, so we are left to wonder about any marginal notes and underlining within, but we certainly know that she thought highly of the book, both because of her words to Betty Hester, ("And have you seen Gilson's book on painting—I can't at the moment recollect the name, but it is very fine and in a paperback")[62] and because of her glowing review, published May 3, 1958, in *The Bulletin*. In the preface Gilson confesses to his reader: "In metaphysics, a purely personal evolution led the author . . . to the rediscovery of the solid, down-to-earth realism of the classical metaphysics of being as interpreted by St. Thomas Aquinas."[63] This reference to 'down-to-earth realism' is an excellent and appropriate description of Hillbilly Thomism, and likely would have appealed to O'Connor. In his next paragraph, Gilson states his thesis as "interpreting the evolution of the art of painting, especially that of its most recent phase, in the light of the classical metaphysics of being."[64] According to O'Connor, "The most valuable part of the book is the discussion of modern painting contained in the last two chapters. The essence of the art of painting is not imitation but the creative addition of artifacts to nature."[65] In the second to last chapter Gilson defends modern painting with a Thomistic argument: "Representational or not, a painting is a true work of art to the extent that it 'abstracts' from all the elements that are not compatible with, or required for, the embodiment in matter of the germinal form conceived by the painter. In a word, because it is identical with the germinal form itself, abstraction is creation."[66] Whether or not Gilson's defense of modern painting as *being good as long as the form of a thing is abstracted and then re-presented by the painter* is valid is beyond the scope of our study, but it is notable that this line of thinking turns up in O'Connor's own writing on narrative art, as when she states, "The storyteller is concerned with what is."[67]

Gilson's Influence on O'Connor

Étienne Gilson influenced Flannery O'Connor in two major ways. Firstly, as a philosopher, a Thomist, and a Catholic, his writings helped O'Connor to understand that her art, a literary expression of Hillbilly Thomism, and Catholic faith were non-competitive in nature. In the final chapter of *Painting and Reality,* Gilson spends a few pages explaining how philosophy, theology, and art work together for the sake of a common good, which would have surely affirmed O'Connor's vocation as narrative artist. Gilson saw theology "acting as a guiding star for philosophers considering the nature of the world as well as for artists considering the nature of art,"[68] and he notes that "all truly creative art is religious in its own right."[69] O'Connor would have found comfort and affirmation in such words, especially as one who considered her "audience [to be] the people who think God is dead."[70] O'Connor was out to engage the modern world as a narrative artist inspired by Thomism, and Gilson's writings offered her the philosophical confidence and assurance that her vision in doing so was clear, reasonable, and necessary.

Secondly—and more to the point of this essay—O'Connor found in Gilson a reliable teacher and guide to help her understand and then navigate the perilous waters of modernity through a detailed explanation of the history of philosophy, specifically in her reading of *History of Christian Philosophy in the Middle Ages, The Unity of Philosophical Experience*, and *Reason and Revelation in the Middle Ages*. These texts all offer O'Connor a deeper knowledge of St. Thomas Aquinas and Thomistic thought in general, as well as a confidence which allowed her to address in her narrative fiction some of the major problems posed by modernity. It is to these specific problems we now turn.

Four Major Themes of Modernity

We have shown that Guardini and Gilson are two of O'Connor's most important philosophical influences in regard to her understanding of and response to modernity. In this section we will consider four major themes of modernity, as understood by either Guardini or Gilson, that are central to O'Connor's own conception of modernity and reflected in her art.

I. The Self as the Center of Existence

The first major theme of modernity for O'Connor is that in

the modern era man replaces God as the center of existence and philosophical study. This move is often referred to as the *turn to the subject*, and although this theme does take time to develop into a full-blown absolutization of human nature—whereby the human being is taken to be the only personal reality in the universe and his subjectivity taken to be the origin and measure of meaning—René Descartes is widely considered to be the one most responsible for initiating this historic philosophical turn. Most philosophers do not think of Descartes as an atheist—he does offer two proofs for God's existence in his *Meditations*—but because he began his project by turning his focus away from the world and in upon his own mind, we can say that he inadvertently lit modernism's long fuse.

We know from Gooch that Descartes was a key figure in O'Connor's Introduction to Modern Philosophy course at GSCW,[71] and that this course relied heavily on his *Discourse on Method*, yet we have no evidence that O'Connor ever read Descartes's *Meditations*. O'Connor's library is short on modern philosophy in general, and contains no primary works by Descartes. However, Gilson dedicates four full chapters[72] to Descartes's philosophy in *The Unity of Philosophical Experience*, and it is almost certain that this work informed O'Connor's thought regarding the Cartesian influence on modernity. It is within the chapter entitled "Cartesian Idealism" that Gilson recounts Descartes's method:

> Up to his time, no philosopher had denied flatly the existence of material things; Descartes himself,

of course, had never entertained any real doubt as to their actual existence; but he was forbidden by his own principles to take it as an established fact. Like the rest, it was in need of being proved, and it could not have been proved at an earlier stage of the deduction. The mind first, God next, then, and only then, the external world. Such was the order.[73]

Again, Descartes was not a theoretical atheist, but his philosophy acted in effect to relativize the influence of scholastic metaphysics and classical ontology, which sought to show all things as derived causally from God. Because his hyperbolic doubt rejected the power of the senses to offer reliable access to the world, his *turn to the self* in order to discover truth became the launching point of modern philosophy and its skepticism about ontological causality. According to Gilson, this turn to the subject had slowly but naturally led to a truly atheistic turn as its implications were drawn out in the works of Kant, Hegel, Comte, and Feuerbach. As the history of modern philosophy continued to unfold, said Gilson, the Cartesian shift that initially could accommodate two rational proofs for God's existence had now given rise to philosophies such as Auguste Comte's positivism which sought to replace God with 'society.' "Humanity," explains Gilson, "became for Comte an object of worship, the positive god, or Great Being, of the new religion whose self-appointed pope he was."[74] Gilson reports that Ludwig Feuerbach then advanced Comte's thought even further, insisting that:

> Man's self-consciousness has no other object than himself; when, therefore, man says God, he actually means man. In short, God has not created man in his own image, but man has created God in his own image and likeness: the worship of man under the name of God is the very essence of religion. . . . Let us convince man that he is the supreme reality, he will no longer look for happiness above himself, but within himself.[75]

Gilson's account of the history of modern philosophy in *The Unity of Philosophical Experience* no doubt influenced O'Connor, especially in regard to her understanding of how Descartes's turn to the subject eventually led to an understanding of man, or the self, as the center of existence.

Although O'Connor would learn from Gilson how Descartes's *dubito* and *cogito* eventually led to thinkers like Comte and Feuerbach replacing God with humanity, the work of Romano Guardini also informed O'Connor's understanding of the turn to the subject. Guardini responded to Descartes and his disciples with the powerful and embodied argument from the fifth-century bishop and philosopher Augustine of Hippo:

> Augustine is no hermit living shut up within himself. A Platonist, he is stimulated by the Eros-charged atmosphere of debate: a rhetorician, he waxes creative through the spiritual-physical process of speech before audience and community. His is no solitary heart; he thrives on friendship. He has the gift

of assimilating the lives and experiences of others. Into the destinies unfolding around him, which he co-experiences, he pours the rich abundance of his own existence, casting it in the different rôles that are to work out his own drama. Augustine's world is no inhuman mechanical system, but an infinite composite of interrelated images and symbols through which gleams the one all-possessing God, who creates in acts of love. Everywhere in the world rules the law of participation. Thus the whole world of Augustinian experience pulses with the life of another into one's own—or the opposite: the flinging of one's life into that of another and living one's self out in it.[76]

Within this quotation Guardini exposes what he found to be the major errors of Cartesian philosophy (i.e., man's isolation and alienation, a mechanistic theory of the universe, and a loveless God) while at the same time offering a satisfying alternative to the weaknesses of Descartes's modern philosophy in the steadfast wisdom of the perennial philosophy found in Augustine.

In this poignant excerpt from O'Connor's essay "Novelist and Believer" we note the influence of Gilson and Guardini:

> There is one type of modern man who recognizes spirit in himself but who fails to recognize a being outside himself whom he can adore as Creator and Lord; consequently he has become his own ultimate

> concern. He says with Swinburne, "Glory to man in the highest, for he is the master of things," or with Steinbeck, "In the end was the word and the word was with men." For him, man has his own natural spirit of courage and dignity and pride and must consider it a point of honor to be satisfied with this.[77]

O'Connor was convinced that one of the major faults of the modern project, if not the most serious fault, is its attempt to replace God as the center of all being with man in his subjectivity, because to her mind this philosophical move results in the very opposite of what it hopes to accomplish. That is, rather than elevating the dignity of humanity, placing humanity and its subjective search for meaning at the center of reality is a philosophical move that asks far too much of a finite creature and eventually results in human beings actually becoming less than what they are. In a letter to Cecil Dawkins dated November 8, 1958, O'Connor explains this philosophical position:

> The notion of the perfectibility of man came about at the time of the Enlightenment in the 18th century.... The Liberal approach is that man has never fallen, never incurred guilt, and is ultimately perfectible by his own efforts. Therefore, evil in this light is a problem of better housing, sanitation, health, etc. and all mysteries will eventually be cleared up. Judgment is out of place because man is not responsible. Of course there are degrees of adherence to this, all sorts of mixtures, but it is the direction the modern heads toward.[78]

According to O'Connor's thought, human beings are incapable of perfecting themselves apart from God. So, modernity's move to replace God with human society, or human conquest of nature, or the creativity of the modern self will always be detrimental to man, causing him far more harm than good, regardless of whether or not such a move will lead to greater material progress for the human race.

II. A Disregard for Mystery

In "Novelist and Believer," O'Connor writes, "The fiction writer presents mystery through manners, grace through nature, but when he finishes there always has to be left over that sense of Mystery which cannot be accounted for by any human formula."[79] O'Connor's understanding of and appreciation for the role of mystery in human living was certainly influenced by her Catholic faith, which constantly references, professes, and celebrates the mystery of God, particularly present in the Incarnation, the Sacraments, and the lives of the saints; but her philosophical understanding of mystery was most likely influenced by her reading of Gabriel Marcel's *The Mystery of Being*.[80] O'Connor describes Marcel as "one of the mystic-existentialist writers in the Church"[81] and mentions him seven times in *The Habit of Being*. Although she admits that she struggled to understand his *Metaphysical Journal*,[82] she did consider *The Mystery of Being* "readable," adding, "No Aristotle in him that I can detect."[83] Marcel's approach to mystery is phenomenological and not Thomistic, for he places a great emphasis on human experience and the "felt presence" of mystery, but he also claims that mystery is forever and always aligned with what he calls "the essential" and that "the nexus between the ideas of Eternity and mystery is as strict a one as can be,"[84] which are claims that few Thomists would reject. Marcel also notes that "every mystery is itself like a river, which flows into the Eternal, as into a sea,"[85] and that mystery is only properly understood by way of philosophical reflection, and not by the exact sciences.[86] Ultimately, for Marcel, the mystery of being is the mystery of God.

It has been argued that mystery is an important theme for O'Connor due in large part to her own experience of suffering lupus, the disease which brought about her father's early death and which was slowly working to bring about her own death from the young age of twenty-five.[87] Marcel addresses the mystery of illness in a way that would have resonated with O'Connor:

> If we place ourselves at a purely objective viewpoint, we can hardly see anything more in illness than the breakdown of an apparatus, but we already know, long before we reach the stage of analysis, that this so-called objective account of the matter is not really true to the facts; for an illness impinges on the being of the person who is ill, and, in the presence of his illness, he has to define his attitude toward it; but this is a kind of fact that can have no equivalent at a purely objective level.[88]

O'Connor's experience of lupus was much more than

simply "the breakdown of an apparatus"—her body—and she knew it. It was this reality of mystery, the experience of some great thing beyond what the hard sciences are capable of measuring, that O'Connor wanted to present in her narrative art.

Since mystery plays such a vital role in O'Connor's understanding of the nature of fiction, it follows that she would be highly critical of any philosophical movement that disregarded mystery, which brings us once again to the figure of René Descartes and to an introduction to the philosophy of Baruch Spinoza. In the following sections, then, we will address four major ideas found in Cartesian and Spinozan philosophy and demonstrate how each idea uniquely contributes to a disregard for mystery.[89]

Mathematical Certitude

In recalling his own educational history, Descartes notes, "Above all I delighted in mathematics, because of the certainty and self-evidence of its reasonings."[90] Inspired by this certainty of mathematics as well as the modern sciences of his day, Descartes sought to establish his entire philosophical system on mathematical knowledge, rejecting the perennial philosophy, namely metaphysics. He writes, "Regarding philosophy, I shall say only this: seeing that it has been cultivated for many centuries by the most excellent minds and yet there is still no point in it which is not disputed and hence doubtful, I was not so presumptuous as to hope to achieve any more in it than others had done."[91] But, in fact, Descartes did go on to present an entirely new way of philosophizing, which aimed at mathematical certitude and consequently failed to account for the metaphysical dimension of reality that leads to God.

Gilson notes that "ever since the fourteenth century there had been men to criticize Aristotle, but Descartes's ambition was quite different: it was to replace him."[92] According to Aristotle there is an unbridgeable gap between *practical knowledge*, which is concerned with things that change, and *theoretical knowledge*, which considers things that do not change.[93] Descartes rejects this Aristotelian distinction and insists that "all the things which come within the scope of human knowledge are interconnected in the same way" and that "there can be nothing too remote to be reached in the end or too well hidden to be discovered."[94] In other words, for Descartes all sciences are one, and certain (mathematical) knowledge comes about through the employment of the one common method. Yet as Gilson rightly notes, "If all sciences are one owing to the unity of their common method, Descartes was not only condemned to knowing all, but to knowing all with an absolute certainty."[95] It is precisely this philosophical move to make all sciences one and to reject the theoretical, the speculative, and the contemplative elements of philosophy that ultimately allows no room for mystery. Michael Gillespie explains how Descartes's method essentially replaces the traditional philosopher (metaphysician) with a new kind of philosopher: "The scientist therefore will be the master not of a single area of knowledge but of all knowledge. His knowledge will thus be a *mathêsis universalis*, a universal science or universal mathematics."[96]

Descartes's method fails to let the object of study determine the method of each science, taking instead the modern observational sciences like mechanics as the basis for the kind of philosophy he wishes to educe, whereas, as Gilson reminds us, "According to Aristotle and the Scholastics, each science was both defined as a distinct branch of knowledge and determined by the nature of its own object."[97] The consequence of rejecting the Aristotelian-Thomistic tradition is that Descartes limits his understanding of knowledge to a mathematical kind of knowledge which results in what Charles Taylor refers to as a "disengagement"[98] with the fullness of reality. An example from O'Connor's fiction will help illustrate this point.

In "The Artificial Nigger," O'Connor presents two white rural dwellers, Mr. Head and his grandson Nelson, who embark on a journey to the city, where they subsequently find themselves lost in a black neighborhood. There is a growing tension between the old man and the boy throughout most of the story until the culminating moment when both characters, exhausted and desperate to return home, find themselves standing before a "plaster figure of a Negro sitting bent over on a low yellow brick fence that curved around a wide lawn."[99] O'Connor describes the moment:

> The two of them stood there with their necks forward at almost the same angle and their shoulders

curved in almost exactly the same way and their hands trembling identically in their pockets. Mr. Head looked like an ancient child and Nelson like a miniature old man. They stood gazing at the artificial Negro as if they were faced with *some great mystery*, some monument to another's victory that brought them together in their common defeat. They could both feel it dissolving their differences like an action of mercy. Mr. Head had never known before what mercy felt like because he had been too good to deserve any, but he felt he knew now. He looked at Nelson and understood that he must say something to the child to show that he was still wise and in the look the boy returned he saw a hungry need for that reassurance. Nelson's eyes seemed to implore him to explain once and for all *the mystery of existence*.[100] (emphasis added)

A Cartesian approach to the world does not allow for the kind of thing that is present in the excerpt above, or, for that matter, what is present in all of O'Connor's fiction. Cartesian philosophy cannot account for the "great mystery" that Mr. Head and Nelson experience in their encounter with the statue, nor can it account for "the mystery of existence" that gives the whole story meaning, for it is precisely this mystery and their encounter with it that allows for the transformation of Mr. Head's character: "He had never thought himself a great sinner before but he saw now his true depravity had been hidden from him lest it cause him despair."[101] Descartes's method is not equipped to account for the mystery of being and therefore displays its own epistemological inadequacy.

Scientism

The second Cartesian idea that brings about a disregard for mystery is related to that of mathematical certitude but is further developed into an outlook we may call *scientism*.[102] We recall that Descartes desired a science that would allow him to know all things with mathematical certainty, and that the first thing that he was certain to know was that he was thinking (the *cogito*).[103] From here he came to know that God exists[104] and eventually he made an argument that the material world also exists, but not in the same manner as it was once thought to exist, for Descartes's method makes a distinction between a thinking thing (*res cogitans*) and extended things (*res extensa*) as the two substances that exist in the world. According to Descartes, the extended world is a purely material world, and therefore knowledge of this material world is of a physical kind, not a metaphysical kind, for the material world is just that, matter without form, so it is studied with physics, not metaphysics. Gilson explains:

> According to St. Thomas Aquinas, the physical order was essentially made up of "natures," that is to say, of active principles, which were the cause of the motions and various operations of their respective matters. In other words, each nature, or form, was essentially an energy, an act. Now it is an obvious fact that such a world was no fit subject

> for a purely mechanical interpretation of physical change; dimensions, positions and distances are by themselves clear things; they can be measured and numbered; but those secret energies that had been ascribed to bodies by Aristotle and St. Thomas, could not be submitted to any kind of calculation. Should they be allowed to stay there, and this indeed was to Descartes the main point, there would remain in nature something confused and obscure, and in science itself a standing element of unintelligibility. As a geometer, who wanted physics to become a department of his universal mathematics, Descartes could not possibly tolerate such a nuisance. Forms, natures and energies had to be eliminated then from the physical world, so that there should be nothing left but extension and an always equal amount of motion caused by God.[105]

Descartes essentially strips the material world of any and all metaphysical meaning, leaving it cold, mechanistic, and disenchanted, but able to be accurately measured by physics and manipulated by man. In fact, Gillespie notes, "the goal of Descartes' scientific project was to make man master and possessor of nature and in this way to prolong human life (perhaps infinitely), to eliminate want, and to provide security."[106] Descartes boldly states his own ambitious goals for his new science here:

> Through this philosophy we could know the power and action of fire, water, air, the stars, the heavens

and all the other bodies in our environment, as distinctly as we know the various crafts of our artisans; and we could use this knowledge—as the artisans use theirs—for all the purposes for which it is appropriate, and thus make ourselves, as it were, the lords and masters of nature. This is desirable not only for the invention of innumerable devices which would facilitate our enjoyment of the fruits of the earth and all the goods we find there, but also, and most importantly, for the maintenance of health, which is undoubtedly the chief good and the foundation of all the other goods in this life. For even the mind depends so much on the temperament and disposition of the bodily organs that if it is possible to find some means of making men in general wiser and more skilful than they have been up till now, I believe we must look for it in medicine. It is true that medicine as currently practised does not contain much of any significant use; but without intending to disparage it, I am sure there is no one, even among its practitioners, who would not admit that all we know in medicine is almost nothing in comparison with what remains to be known, and that we might free ourselves from innumerable diseases, both of the body and of the mind, and perhaps even from the infirmity of old age, if we had sufficient knowledge of their causes and of all the remedies that nature has provided.[107]

What we find in this section of Descartes's *Discourse* is a theme foundational to modernity: the mastery of nature by science. And since according to Descartes the world is without actual natures and is simply material and simply extended, it follows that the best action for human beings is to use their scientific knowledge to become masters of this material world. Richard Kennington notes, "Physics must henceforth abandon final causes, and neither from God nor nature can be derived by rational procedures that knowledge of moral duties which might impede, or guide, the quest for mastery of nature."[108] Ultimately, this Cartesian abandonment of causes and natures leaves the external world as a meaningless set of physical engagements to be studied by the hard sciences but with no place for mystery.

Cogito

Whereas mathematical certitude and scientism both characterize Descartes's posture toward the external world, the *cogito* relates to the internal world of reason and spirit of the thinking subject. This sharp divide between *res cogitans* and *res extensa*, between the world of the mind and the material world, presents some philosophical problems, particularly in light of our discussion of the role of mystery (or lack thereof) in human living according to Descartes's method.

Descartes's *cogito* makes a major break from the Aristotelian-Thomistic tradition in that it denies the body-soul composite of the human being and rather identifies the person simply as one's mind or consciousness. Gilson notes, "As the soul is nothing but thought, so also the body is nothing but extension in space according to the three dimensions. Metaphysics then is pure spiritualism, and physics pure mechanism."[109] According to Aristotle and Thomas, *being* is the bridge that allows man to understand himself in relation to God and the world, but since Descartes's method understands the world as purely mechanistic, God as an idea, and the human person as simply a mind (not at all concerned with the question of being), a paradigm shift ensues. Taylor explains, "The Cartesian subject had lost the kind of depth which belonged to a 'nature' which was part of a cosmic order, where the discovery of what I really am requires that I come to grasp this nature by studying the orders of human social life and the cosmos."[110] The *cogito* finds itself stuck, due to the bifurcation of the internal and external world, in that it is unable to do the sorts of things that once came naturally to the Aristotelian and the Thomist, particularly in regard to the good and the true.

Descartes's *cogito* is animated by freedom[111] and longs for meaning, but is resigned to find freedom and any meaning within itself as a thinking thing, rather than as a body-soul composite turned outward toward God and the world. According to Descartes, God is no longer found outside of one's self and the world is no longer enchanted with natures but is simply reduced to extension. Taylor argues that "mechanism undermines enchantment, the expression-embodiment of higher reality in the things which surround us, and thus made the presence of God in the cosmos something which was no longer experience-near, or at least not at all in the same way. God's power was no longer something you could feel or see in the old way."[112]

For Flannery O'Connor, to speak of mystery is to speak of God's action in the world, but the *cogito* leaves no room for speaking of such action because according to the *cogito* no such world exists.[113]

Naturalism

We have no evidence that Flannery O'Connor ever read any books or articles written by Baruch Spinoza, but she would have been familiar with Gilson's account of his thought in *The Unity of Philosophical Experience*. Gilson introduces Spinoza as one of Descartes's three metaphysical successors—Leibniz and Melebranche are the other two— and explains that "he decided that thought and extension were two attributes of one and the same infinite substance, flowing from that substance with the same necessity, and according to the same law, so that every mode of extension had to find its equivalent in a corresponding mode of thought."[114] The consequence of such thought is ultimately to equate God with nature (*Deus sive natura*),[115] which became known as the philosophical movement of *naturalism*.

Philosophical historian and Spinozan scholar Jonathan Israel argues that Baruch Spinoza's influence on the European Radical Enlightenment has been understated,[116] and that in order to rightly understand modernity, one must go through Spinoza. Gilson explains that Spinoza was "intent upon working out some answer to the Cartesian problem of the 'communication of substances,'"[117] that is, finding some way to bridge the gap between Descartes's *res cogitans* and *res extensa*. Spinoza's solution was to abandon Descartes's distinction altogether and propose that the universe is comprised of one substance, which is God (or nature).[118] According to Spinoza, "there can be only one substance and therefore only one set of rules governing the whole of the reality which surrounds us and of which we are part."[119] The consequence of this teaching is an outright rejection of the supernatural as understood by Thomas and the scholastics; Spinoza's God (or nature) cannot be an agent who freely acts to bring about some end for his creation, such that "things could have been produced by God in no other way, and in no other order, than they have been produced."[120] Moreover, "by negating God's Will and Intelligence, Spinoza leaves no room for traditional notions of divine Providence."[121] This philosophical movement soon flooded Europe in a variety of expressions, all commonly grouped together under the name of its founder. Israel explains:

> [T]he term 'Spinosisme' as used in the French Enlightenment, or *Spinozisterey*, as it was called in Germany, was frequently employed . . . rather broadly to denote virtually the whole of the Radical Enlightenment, that is, all deistic, Naturalistic, and atheistic systems that exclude divine Providence, Revelation, and miracles, including reward and punishment in the hereafter, rather than strict adherence to Spinoza's system as such.[122]

Although, as we have noted, O'Connor was not familiar with Spinozan thought *per se*, she was familiar with naturalism as a philosophical movement, or, at the very least, its consequences. She notes:

> [T]he chief difference between the novelist who is an orthodox Christian and the novelist who is merely a naturalist is that the Christian novelist lives in a larger universe. He believes that the natural world contains the supernatural. And this doesn't mean that his obligation to portray the natural is less; it means it is greater.[123]

And in a letter to Dr. T. R. Spivey dated October 19, 1958, O'Connor writes:

> I suppose what bothers us so much about writing about the return of modern people to a sense of the Holy Spirit is that the religious sense seems to be bred out of them in the kind of society we've lived in since the 18th century. And it's bred out of them double quick now by the religious substitutes for religion. There's nowhere to latch on to, in the characters or the audience. If there were in the public just a slight sense of ordinary theology (much less crisis theology), if they only believed at least that God has the power to do certain things. There is no sense of the power of God that could produce the Incarnation and the Resurrection. They are all so busy explaining away the virgin birth and such things, reducing everything to human proportions that in time they lose even the

sense of the human itself, what they were aiming to reduce everything to.[124]

According to Israel it was Spinoza, "by far the best-known denier of miracles,"[125] who was most responsible for the movement O'Connor acknowledges in the quote above. For Spinoza "there is no difference between an 'event contrary to nature' and a supernatural event."[126] He also believed religion to be "at bottom a psychological procedure, natural in origin and thought-processes, which became transformed into 'superstition' and set down deep roots in men's minds."[127] Although O'Connor may not have known its origins, she certainly did observe the Spinozan philosophical influence:

> One of the effects of modern liberal Protestantism has been gradually to turn religion into poetry and therapy, to make truth vaguer and vaguer and more and more relative, to banish intellectual distinctions, to depend on feeling instead of thought, and gradually to come to believe that God has no power, that he cannot communicate with us, cannot reveal himself to us, indeed has not done so, and that religion is our own sweet invention.[128]

It is not difficult to see that Spinozan philosophy leaves little to no room for mystery, as the only sort of mysteries present in the natural world according to Spinoza are those left to be solved by the natural sciences. Of course, O'Connor thought the opposite is true: "I think the more you write, the less inclined you will be to rely on theories like determinism. Mystery isn't something that is gradually evaporating. It grows along with knowledge."[129]

III. A General Distrust of the Concrete

The next major theme for our consideration is rather ancient in its origins, but experienced a great revival in modernity beginning with Descartes's project. *Gnosticism* or *Spiritualism* or *Mentalism* is a philosophical movement that prioritizes ideas over things; it is the other side of Descartes's scientistic/mechanistic view of the external world. When the physical world becomes the sole purview of the hard sciences, the inner world of the *cogito* becomes a world of rational constructions and *a priori* ideas, where perceptions of God, the self, freedom, truth, etc., are not grounded in the world of natures but grounded in notions formulated by the subject. Gilson presents it in this way:

> Let us therefore state this first principle, whose consequence will run not only through the whole body of Cartesian philosophy, but through the whole body of modern idealism as well: all that can be clearly and distinctly known as belonging to the idea of a thing can be said of the thing itself. As a matter of fact, it *is* the thing. [130]

Because Descartes's method is based upon mathematical certainty, and because "mathematicians deal with nothing but ideas,"[131] it follows that, according to his system, priority would always be given to ideas, not things. Guardini makes this observation: "Thus, founded on scientific knowledge, modern 'pure' spirituality comes into being, soon to deteriorate to a mere abstract conceptualism. The result is a completely isolated inwardness, and with it comes the question whether, and, if at all, to what extent, it will be able to express itself."[132] O'Connor recognized this preference for ideas and the tendency toward prioritizing the spiritual (apart from the material) as a dangerous philosophical position that rejects reality because it ignores how things actually are. She writes:

> The Manicheans separated spirit and matter. To them all material things were evil. They sought pure spirit and tried to approach the infinite directly without any mediation of matter. This is also pretty much the modern spirit, and for the sensibility infected with it, fiction is hard if not impossible to write because fiction is so very much an incarnational art.[133]

One of the gravest consequences of this Cartesian-inspired concept of the self is the abandonment of the human body, whose mediation of knowledge concretely through the senses is in the Thomistic tradition an essential part of what it means to be human. Following Aristotle, Aquinas teaches that human knowledge begins with the senses (*principium nostrae cognitionis est a sensu*)[134] and we can trust that the information our senses convey about *what-is* is both true and intelligible. A philosophy that abandons the body as the way man naturally comes to know the world is a philosophy that essentially abandons humanity for a new conception of the "true self." Gilson explains:

> Descartes' conception of man as an angel, or disembodied thinking substance, swept Europe, and was soon received as immediate evidence by the greatest thinkers of his time. Stripping themselves both of their bodies and of their souls, they became magnificent minds who, theoretically at least, did not feel indebted to their bodies for any one of their ideas.[135]

One major consequence of this new understanding of the "true self" as mind or spirit is that, according to Guardini, "man grows more and more dependent on himself, utilizing the given materials in nature, life, and the psyche for the creation of a form of existence which he himself has designed and willed."[136] Such a notion of the human person as dis-embodied and essentially self-creating has profound philosophical implications, particularly for the Catholic, as we will see at the end of this section.

Flannery O'Connor outright rejected any Gnostic approach to reality that bypasses the senses and the material world, because she agreed with St. Thomas that knowledge begins in the senses and reality is found within the concrete, not apart from it. In particular, she was wholly convinced that her narrative art was dependent upon the concrete, as "fiction operates through the senses."[137] Throughout her essay "Writing Short Stories," O'Connor vehemently rejects all notions of Cartesian spiritualism and Gnosticism in favor of a Thomistic approach to reality that begins with the senses, forever insisting on the importance of acknowledging the concrete in human knowing. We note the distinction she makes between what we might call a *concrete* writer and an *abstract* writer:

> Now this is a very humble level to have to begin on, and most people who think they want to write stories are not willing to start there. They want to write about problems, not people; or about abstract issues, not concrete situations. They have an idea of a feeling, or an overflowing ego, or they want to Be A Writer, or they want to give their wisdom to the world in a simple-enough way for the world to be able to absorb it. In any case, they don't have a story and they wouldn't be willing to write it if they did, and in the absence of a story, they set out to find a theory or a formula or a technique.[138]

O'Connor's Hillbilly Thomism is on full display in this quotation, as she insists on an acceptance of reality as given through the concrete, and she rejects any and all attempts to replace reality with abstract ideas or formulas. For O'Connor, the imperative for narrative art is to "Show these things and you don't have to say them," which is to say storytelling must focus on reality and not simply ideas[139]. She must reject the spiritualism of Descartes in particular, and modernity in general, because it is an affront to art. Perhaps the best example of this principle is O'Connor's explanation of why separating the theme (idea) of a story from the story itself (concrete reality) fails:

> When you can state the theme of a story, when you can separate it from the story itself, then you can be

> sure the story is not a very good one. The meaning of a story has to be embodied in it, has to be made concrete in it. A story is a way to say something that can't be said any other way, and it takes every word in the story to say what the meaning is. You tell a story because a statement would be inadequate. When anybody asks what a story is about, the only proper thing is to tell him to read the story. The meaning of fiction is not abstract meaning but experienced meaning, and the purpose of making statements about the meaning of a story is only to help you to experience that meaning more fully.
>
> Fiction is an art that calls for the strictest attention to the real—whether the writer is writing a naturalistic story or a fantasy. I mean that we always begin with what is or with what has an eminent possibility of truth about it. Even when one writes a fantasy, reality is the proper basis of it.[140]

In *The Lord*, Romano Guardini writes, "What have we to do with the spiritualism of Gnostics?—the answer is: A great deal! Modernity is often completely confused by 'spiritualism.'"[141] O'Connor agrees; her critique of modernity's confusion—whether the rejection of concrete reality operates under the name of spiritualism, Gnosticism, Manicheanism, or Mentalism—is ultimately a metaphysical and epistemological critique. She thought that this philosophical rejection of the concrete produced unfortunate consequences not only within society, but also within the Church, for "in the last four or five centuries, Catholics have overemphasized the abstract and consequently impoverished their imaginations and their capacity for prophetic insight."[142]

Robert George has written extensively on how this Cartesian understanding of the subjective, disembodied self continues to hold influence over culture in the twenty-first century. The introduction to George's celebrated essay "Gnostic Liberalism" is worthy of our consideration, particularly because he explains why Catholicism should forever and always be critical of the Cartesian-inspired understanding of the "true self" and because he shows the consequences of this philosophical movement:

> Christianity's rejection of body-self dualism answered the challenge to orthodoxy posed by what was known as "Gnosticism." Gnosticism comprised a variety of ideologies, some ascetical, others quite the opposite. What they held in common was an understanding of the human being—an anthropology—that sharply divides the material or bodily, on the one hand, and the spiritual or mental or affective, on the other. For Gnostics, it was the immaterial, the mental, the affective that ultimately matters. Applied to the human person, this means that the material or bodily is inferior—if not a prison to escape, certainly a mere instrument to be manipulated to serve the goals of the "person," understood as the spirit or mind or psyche. The self is a spiritual or mental substance; the body, its merely material vehicle. You and I, as persons, are identified entirely with the spirit or mind or psyche,

and not at all (or in only the most highly attenuated sense) with the body that we occupy (or are somehow "associated with") and use.

Against such dualism, the anti-Gnostic position asserts a view of the human person as a dynamic unity: a personal body, a bodily self. This rival vision is found throughout the Hebrew Scriptures and Christian teaching. This is not to suggest that Christian teaching rules out the view that the individual is numerically identical with his or her immaterial soul. Contemporary Christian thinkers are divided on whether the separated soul is numerically distinct from the human person, or is just the person in radically mutilated form. They agree, however, on the essential point, namely, that the body is no mere extrinsic instrument of the human person (or "self"), but is an integral part of the personal reality of the human being. Christ is resurrected bodily....

So we are animals—rational animals, to be sure, but not pure minds or intellects. Our personal identity across time consists in the endurance of the animal organisms we are. From this follows a crucial proposition: The human person comes to be when the human organism does, and survives—as a person—at least until the organism ceases to be.

Yet we are not brute animals. We are animals with a rational nature—organized from the start for conceptual thought, and for practical deliberation, judgment, and choice. These intellectual powers are not reducible to the purely material. Creatures possessing them are able, with maturity and under favoring circumstances, to grasp intelligible (not just sensible) features of options for action, and to respond to those reasons with choices not determined by antecedent events. It is not that we act arbitrarily or randomly, but that we choose based on judgments of value that incline us toward different options without compelling us. There is no contradiction, on the hylomorphic view, between our animality and our rationality.[143]

Flannery O'Connor was convinced that any attempt to separate the spiritual world from the material world is to meddle with our perception of reality in a way that causes harm, not only to one's art, but also to the human person, and hence the human community. Being a narrative artist and not a philosopher, O'Connor may not have been able to articulate the current state of affairs with the philosophical precision of George, but we have good reason to believe that she would have agreed with him, on the evidence found in her fiction as well as in her own life's witness.[144]

IV. The Subordination of Reason

Closely related to modernity's attraction to spiritualism and its aversion to concrete reality are the philosophical movements of sentimentalism[145] and voluntarism,[146] both of which thrive in a modern universe of meaninglessness, driven by the individual subject. O'Connor had some significant Thomistic critiques of sentimentalism and voluntarism, primarily because these movements displace reason's proper and privileged role in human living,[147] but before turning to the words of O'Connor, we will first look to O'Connor's sources in the writings of Gilson and Guardini.

In *The Unity of Philosophical Experience* Gilson surprisingly addresses the topic of sentimentalism in a chapter entitled "The Sociologism of A. Comte." Auguste Comte is known as "the originator of sociology and 'positivism,' a philosophical system by which he aimed to discover and perfect the proper political arrangements of modern industrial society."[148] Michel Bourdeau explains Comte's project:

> Its goal is the reorganization of society. Science gets involved only after politics, when Comte suggests calling in scientists to achieve that goal. So, while science plays a central role in positive polity, positivism is anything but a blind admiration for science. From 1847, positivism is placed under the 'continuous dominance of the heart' (*la prépondérance continue du coeur*), and the motto 'Order and Progress' becomes 'Love as principle, order as basis, progress as end' (*L'amour pour principe, l'ordre pour base et le progrès pour but*). This turn, unexpected for many of his contemporaries, was in fact well motivated and is characteristic of the very dynamics of Comte's thought.[149]

Although one may not readily associate positivism with sentimentalism, or Comte with sentimentalism, Gilson does, because he thought that Comte's project ultimately results in the subordination of reason, a consequence of his rejection of metaphysics.[150] This result is ironic, because in striving for scientific objectivity, Comte's project "invariably culminates in the capitulation of science itself to some irrational element."[151]

Gilson writes, "There was nothing wrong in discovering sociology . . . The only trouble with Comte was that, after having conceived the possibility of such a science, he thought that he could achieve it all alone; and that, having more or less achieved it, he asked it to solve all philosophical problems."[152] As with every chapter in *Unity*, Gilson presents a movement that attempts to replace metaphysics as first philosophy, and then shows how such an attempt fails, as "philosophy always buries its undertakers."[153] For Gilson, Comte's project failed because it "reached a point at which reason had nothing more to say," since his project was based not on "reason, but a feeling."[154] Gilson calls this project "sentimentalism," which subordinates the intellect to the heart,[155] citing Comte's motto, "We tire of thinking and even of acting; we never tire of loving."[156] In the Thomistic tradition, feelings, emotions, passions, or what Comte calls 'the heart' are important, as they make up a necessary part of what it means to be human,[157] but they are always subordinate to the intellect, for the intellect is the higher power and it is responsible for controlling and directing its subordinates. Comte's project attempts to prioritize feeling or "love" over intellect, claiming, "both speculation and action are dominated by affection and that social consensus depends on the affective life,"[158] not the intelligent life, which ultimately results in his particular brand of sentimentalism.[159] In summary, in a positivistic world of mere mechanical dead physical objects, without any clear transcendent origin, the atheism of Comte moves away from the rationalism of Descartes toward a despair of any transcendent meaning and a celebration of subjective sentiment.

Although Guardini's *The Spirit of the Liturgy* is absent from O'Connor's personal library, it is probable that O'Connor was familiar with this classic work. In the final chapter, entitled "The Primacy of the Logos over the Ethos," Guardini makes an important distinction between the Middle Ages and Modernity:

> It is safe to affirm that the Middle Ages, in philosophy at least, answered the question as to the relation between these two fundamental principles by decisively ranking knowledge before will and the activity attendant upon the functioning of the latter. They gave the Logos precedence over the Ethos . . . this stands out as the fundamental attitude of the Middle Ages, which took the Hereafter as the constant and exclusive goal of all earthly striving.
>
> Modern times brought about a great change. The great objective institutions of the Middle Ages—class solidarity, the municipalities, the Empire—broke up. The power of the Church was no longer, as

> formerly, absolute and temporal. In every direction individualism became more strongly pronounced and independent. This development was chiefly responsible for the growth of scientific criticism, and in a special manner the criticism of knowledge itself. The inquiry into the essence of knowledge, which formally followed a constructive method, now assumes, as a result of the profound spiritual changes which have taken place, its characteristic critical form. Knowledge itself becomes questionable, and as a result the center of gravity and the fulcrum of the spiritual life gradually shifts from knowledge to the will.[160]

The prioritization of the will over the intellect in the free modern subject as an act of subjectivity (an inversion, as Guardini describes, of the medieval prioritization of the intellect over the will) is known as *voluntarism*.[161] It is a major philosophical move, and problematic according to Guardini because, like sentimentalism, voluntarism replaces the highest power of a human being with a subordinate power and then expects the subordinate power to do the work that by its very nature it is incapable of doing. Guardini explains:

> The will is not required to prove truth, nor is the latter obliged to give an account of itself to the will, but the will has to acknowledge itself as perfectly incompetent before truth. It does not create the latter, but finds it. The will has to admit that it is blind and needs the light, the leadership, and the

organizing formative power of truth. It must admit as a fundamental principle the primacy of knowledge over the will, of the Logos over the Ethos.[162]

Guardini observed that voluntarism leads to the prioritization of the practical over the metaphysical as well as to the prioritization of the active life over the contemplative life. He understood these philosophical moves as dangerous, not because he thought that practical matters and human action are unimportant, but because he thought that the presumption that the will is capable of doing the kind of work that is proper to the intellect ultimately leads to disastrous and unintended consequences.[163] Guardini explains, "This presumption is guilty of having put modern man into the position of a blind person groping his way in the dark, because the fundamental force upon which it has based life—the will—is blind. The will can function and produce, but cannot see. From this is derived the restlessness which nowhere finds tranquility."[164]

Flannery O'Connor does not use the word *voluntarism*, but she was very aware of philosophical problems that emerge when the intellect is refused its rightful place in human living, and she knew that it is the intellect that guides the will, and not the other way around. We see a fitting example of this principle at work in the following excerpt from O'Connor's prayer journal:

> You say, dear God, to ask for grace and it will be given. I ask for it. I realize that there is more to it than that—that I have to behave like I want it. "Not those

who say, Lord, Lord, but those who do the Will of My Father." Please help me to know the will of my Father—not a scrupulous nervousness nor yet a lax presumption but a clear, reasonable knowledge; and after this give me a strong Will to be able to bend it to the Will of the Father.[165]

We note the order of things according to O'Connor: First, she asks *to know* the will of her Father, and the kind of knowledge that she desires is "clear" and "reasonable." Such is the work of the intellect. Second, she asks God *to give her a strong will* and the ability to bend this will to God's will for her. Such is the work of the will. The intellect and the will work together, according to O'Connor, but priority is given to the intellect, which, in turn, guides the will.

Regarding sentimentalism, O'Connor was very familiar with the term and used it frequently as a way of describing an inability to see reality for what it is. In "The Church and the Fiction Writer," she writes: "sentimentality is an excess, a distortion of sentiment usually in the direction of an overemphasis on innocence, and that innocence, wherever it is overemphasized in the ordinary human condition, tends by some natural law to become its opposite."[166] O'Connor distrusted feelings or emotions to tell the truth about reality because it is the job of the intellect to know reality, and while emotions and feelings and the passions of the soul are an important part of human living, for O'Connor they were always subordinate to the intellect, as we can only make sense of emotions and feelings with the help of the intellect.

Perhaps the best example of O'Connor's understanding of the priority of reason in response to sentimentalism is found in her letter to Betty Hester dated September 6, 1955:

> But I can never agree with you that the Incarnation, or any truth, has to satisfy emotionally to be right (and I would not agree that for the natural man the Incarnation does not satisfy emotionally). It does not satisfy emotionally for the person brought up under many forms of false intellectual discipline such as 19th-century mechanism, for instance. Leaving the Incarnation aside, the very notion of God's existence is not emotionally satisfactory anymore for great numbers of people, which does not mean that God ceases to exist. M. Sartre finds God emotionally unsatisfactory in the extreme, as do most of my friends of less stature than he. The truth does not change according to our ability to stomach it emotionally... I must say that the thought of everyone lolling about in an emotionally satisfying faith is repugnant to me. I believe that we are ultimately directed Godward but that this journey is often impeded by emotion. I don't think you are a jellyfish. But I suspect you of being a Romantic.[167]

Although romanticism[168] differs from sentimentalism and voluntarism, O'Connor found a common philosophical thread in all three movements: they each displace the primacy of reason. As a Hillbilly Thomist she was convinced that any philosophical position that attempts to replace reason with a subordinate human power ultimately fails.

O'Connor's most notable critique of such a philosophical position is found in her "Introduction to A Memoir of Mary Ann":

> In this popular pity, we mark our gain in sensibility and our loss in vision. If other ages felt less, they saw more, even though they saw with the blind, prophetical, unsentimental eye of acceptance, which is to say, of faith. In the absence of this faith now, we govern by tenderness. It is a tenderness which, long since cut off from the person of Christ, is wrapped in theory. When tenderness is detached from the source of tenderness, its logical outcome is terror. It ends in the forced-labor camps and in the fumes of the gas chamber.[169]

As insistent as O'Connor was on the need to avoid the subordination of the intellect to any other power, this insistence does not make O'Connor a stoic, for she certainly recognized the place of feelings and emotions in human living, but she was always quick to insist that the intellect must never be subordinated, for its job is to guide and govern the passions of the soul.[170]

Wise Blood as an Artistic Rendering of O'Connor's Vision of Modernity

Now that we have noted some key ways in which Guardini and Gilson have influenced O'Connor's philosophical vision of modernity and have examined four major philosophical movements that clarify that vision, we turn to O'Connor's first novel, *Wise Blood*, in order to show how the four major philosophical themes outlined above become manifest in her narrative art.[171]

The Church of Christ Without Christ

The protagonist of *Wise Blood* is twenty-two-year-old Hazel Motes, a soldier who has just returned home after fighting in a war on the other side of the world. Motes is from Eastrod, Tennessee, but he is on his way to Taulkinham, which according to Christina Bieber Lake "symbolizes the modern world."[172] He is the grandson of a preacher, and therefore has what O'Connor calls "wise blood," meaning that, like his grandfather, Hazel has received a prophetic call to serve the Lord.

> His grandfather had traveled three counties in a Ford automobile. Every fourth Saturday he had driven into Eastrod as if he were just in time to save them all from Hell, and he was shouting before he had the car door open. People gathered around his Ford because he seemed to dare them to. He would climb up on the nose of it and preach from there and sometimes

> he would climb onto the top of it and shout down at them. They were like stones! he would shout. But Jesus had died to redeem them! Jesus was so soul-hungry that He had died, one death for all, but He would have died every soul's death for one! Did they understand that? Did they understand that for each stone soul, He would have died ten million deaths, had His arms and legs stretched on the cross and nailed ten million times for one of them?[173]

For most of the novel, Hazel runs from his prophetic calling and his wise blood, going so far as to become a preacher of the anti-Gospel, founding his own church:

> "Well, I preach the Church Without Christ. I'm a member and preacher to that church where the blind don't see and the lame don't walk and what's dead stays that way. Ask me about that church and I'll tell you it's the church that the blood of Jesus don't foul with redemption..."
>
>   Listen, you people, I'm going to take the truth with me wherever I go," Haze called. "I'm going to preach it to whoever'll listen at whatever place. I'm going to preach there was no Fall because there was nothing to fall from and no Redemption and no Judgment because there wasn't the first two. Nothing matters but that Jesus was a liar."[174]

We have noted that a major mark of modernity, according to O'Connor, is the turn to the subject whereby the self takes priority over God, whereby man becomes the center of existence and reality. There is no mistaking O'Connor's intention in her presentation of Hazel Motes as an embodiment of that modern spirit. He outright rejects the Gospel he has been called to preach and instead creates his own anti-Gospel proclaimed in the Church Without Christ, a Comtean dream.[175] Motes places himself at the center of things and presents himself as the one with the authority to tell the truth, which he will preach to whoever will listen. He seeks his freedom not by following God's commandments, but by breaking them, making himself the measure of all things, insisting that "the only way to the truth is through blasphemy."[176] In *Wise Blood*, Hazel Motes plays foil to Augustine. As Guardini notes, "Augustine experiences himself and the world as real, but as constantly realized by God. And he experiences deeply the fact that he is and lives, that everything is significant, drawing its power and significance, however, from God's presence and efficacy in it."[177] Augustine finds himself at home in the world once he finds himself in relationship with God, whereas Motes finds himself alienated in a seemingly meaningless physical cosmos centered on human freedom. Rather than turn to God to relieve his alienation, Motes turns to founding his own church, the Church Without Christ, which only increases his experience of alienation. It is no doubt an exaggerated and comical presentation of modernity's turn to the subject, but O'Connor thinks such exaggeration is most necessary:

> When you can assume that your audience holds the same beliefs you do, you can relax a little and use

more normal means of talking to it; when you have to assume that it does not, then you have to make your vision apparent by shock—to the hard of hearing you shout, and for the almost-blind you draw large and startling figures.[178]

Hazel Motes, then, is an embodiment of modernity for O'Connor insofar as he rejects God and the authority of sacred scripture and instead looks to himself as the center of meaning, preaching his new Gospel to anyone who will listen. Bieber Lake observes: "Haze becomes the quintessential inheritor of the *cogito ergo sum*—I think; therefore, I am. The further he moves from the life of the body in Eastrod to the life of the mind in 'Talking'ham, the more firmly he believes in modern philosophy's next step: 'I think; therefore, the world can be as I think.'"[179] According to Guardini, this Cartesian mode of thinking is anti-Augustinian, for according to Augustine, "Thinking, waiting, man probes the meaning of things. Via the thing, he comes to the idea behind it; via the idea, to God, and in God to himself."[180] O'Connor's critique of Descartes, therefore, is on display both in the character of Hazel Motes and in his Church Without Christ.

Enoch Emery's De-evolution
The character of Enoch Emery[181] in *Wise Blood* is important to our study for two major reasons. First, Enoch embodies *de-evolution* or *birth-in-reverse*, which is a manifestation of the naturalism we noted above. Second, Enoch Emory is the one who discovers *the new jesus* of Hazel Motes's

Church Without Christ and presents him to Haze, which is a turning point in the novel.

The first mention of Enoch Emery in *Wise Blood* is as "a damp-haired pimpled boy" who had "yellow hair and a fox-shaped face."[182] A few pages later O'Connor writes, "He looked like a friendly hound dog with light mange" and she notes his "panting."[183] O'Connor's language is deliberate, as she presents Enoch as a symbol of de-evolution from human to animal. Enoch works at City Forest Park, which is symbolic of the wildness of nature, rather than the civility of man. He crawls around in the bushes and watches women sunbathe, seeing them not as persons with dignity but simply as objects to satisfy his animal instincts.[184] O'Connor has him say things like, "Well, I'll be dog,"[185] and she describes him crawling out of the bushes "on all fours."[186] There is no mistaking what O'Connor is doing with Enoch Emery; his character reveals what humanity becomes in modernity when God and the mystery of the human person (as created in God's image and likeness), are rejected. Guardini's influence seems to be on display here, as O'Connor presents the Augustinian perspective of a human being craving to be animalistic as an escape from responsibility and a drive toward the primacy of subjective will and sentiment.[187] Bieber Lake notes, "the primal, mythic, and earthy grotesquerie of *Wise Blood* metaphorically depicts the moral degradation of man who denies God, is blind to his own depravity, and is given over to lust."[188] It is true that Hazel Motes is also given over to lust, but ultimately he is saved from it, whereas Enoch

Emory continues to degrade and devolve until he becomes an animal.

In one of the more humorous scenes in the novel, Enoch makes his way to the city and comes across a sign at the local theater:

> He found himself facing a life-size four-color picture of a gorilla. Over the gorilla's head, written in red letters was, "GONGA! Giant Jungle Monarch and a Great Star! Here in Person!!!" At the level of the gorilla's knee, there was more that said, "Gonga will appear in person in front of this theatre at 12 a.m. TODAY! A free pass to the first ten brave enough to step up and shake his hand!"[189]

Enoch is excited to meet this movie star gorilla, but he lacks self-awareness and fails to recognize that this meet-and-greet with Gonga is for children, while he himself is a young adult. "A child asked him how old he was. Another observed that he had funny-looking teeth. He ignored all this as best he could and began to straighten out the umbrella."[190] Enoch is oblivious. His inability to see the awkwardness of the situation is symbolic of his turning from the life of reason to a life guided primarily by his animal passions. To us readers, it is unclear if, as he stands in line, Enoch understands that Gonga is actually a human being dressed in an ape costume rather than a real ape. He, the lone adult, appears more excited to meet Gonga than any of the children surrounding him:

> There were only two children in front of him by now.

The first one shook hands and stepped aside. Enoch's heart was beating violently. The child in front of him finished and stepped aside and left him facing the ape, who took his hand with an automatic motion.

It was the first hand that had been extended to Enoch since he had come to the city. It was warm and soft.

For a second he only stood there, clasping it. Then he began to stammer. "My name is Enoch Emery," he mumbled. "I attended the Rodemill Boys Bible Academy. I work at the city zoo. I seen two of your pictures. I'm only eighteen year old but I already work for the city. My daddy made me com . . ." and his voice cracked.

The star leaned slightly forward and a change came in his eyes: an ugly pair of human ones moved closer and squinted at Enoch from behind the celluloid pair. "You go to hell," a surly voice inside the ape-suit said, low but distinctly, and the hand was jerked away.

Enoch's humiliation was so sharp and painful that he turned around three times before he realized which direction he wanted to go in. Then he ran off into the rain as fast as he could.[191]

Eventually Enoch makes his way back into the city and finds the van that carried Gonga parked across the street from another theater.[192] He enters the back of the truck, and shortly after, Gonga too climbs in while the driver gets into the cab and drives off. Soon there is a major scuffle in the back of the van, the driver unaware of "certain thumping noises, not those of the normal gorilla . . . drowned out by the drone of the motor and the steady sound of wheels against the road."[193] Enoch murders the actor, steals the gorilla suit, jumps out of the back of the van when it slows down at a train crossing, and runs off into the woods. He buries his clothes in the ground and puts on the gorilla suit. Symbolically Enoch has returned to his natural animal state, in the woods, in the image and likeness of a gorilla.

> For a time after this, it stood very still and didn't do anything. Then it began to growl and beat its chest; it jumped up and down and flung its arms and thrust its head forward. The growls were thin and uncertain at first but they grew louder after a second. They became low and poisonous, louder again, low and poisonous again . . . No gorilla in existence, whether in the jungles of Africa or California, or in New York City in the finest apartment in the world, was happier at that moment than this one, whose god had finally rewarded it.[194]

Once Enoch devolves into a beast, O'Connor intentionally refers to him only as 'it' for the remainder of the novel. Enoch Emory and the mystery of his human person are lost and his regression to an animal state is now complete.

The second major component of our study of Enoch Emory's character in regard to a devaluation of mystery takes place before he transforms into a beast.[195] Enoch has been listening to Hazel Motes preaching about his Church

Without Christ and his new jesus:

> What you need is something to take the place of Jesus, something that would speak plain. The Church Without Christ don't have a Jesus but it needs one! It needs a new jesus! It needs one that's all man, without blood to waste, and it needs one that don't look like any other man so you'll look at him. Give me such a jesus, you people. Give me such a new jesus and you'll see how far the Church Without Christ can go![196]

Enoch recalls seeing a shriveled-up mummy at the local museum and thinks that this artifact can be the new jesus for Haze's Church Without Christ. He disguises himself in blackface, a black beard, and glasses and makes his way into the museum. Enoch takes the "shriveled man" out of the display case and shoves him in a paper bag, sneaks past the security guard, and eventually makes his way over to Hazel Motes's apartment with the mummy tucked under his arm. O'Connor writes:

> He couldn't understand at all why he had let himself risk his skin for a dead shriveled-up part-nigger dwarf that had never done anything but get himself embalmed and then lain stinking in a museum the rest of his life. It was far beyond his understanding. He was very sullen. So far as he was now concerned, one jesus was as bad as another.[197]

Jesus Christ, understood by orthodox Christianity to be true God and true man in the mystery of the Incarnation, is here being replaced by a mummy. We have shown above that a position commonly held in modern Enlightenment authors is that even if God exists, he cannot do anything that would encroach upon the natural order. Here O'Connor presents the new jesus, not even as a living man, but a dead man, which, Thomistically speaking, is not even a man, but a corpse.[198] The mystery of God and the mystery of the Incarnation are rejected completely and what is embraced is an ancient corpse; symbolically it is humanity without a soul.

Soon, Enoch takes the mummy to Hazel's apartment and hands the wet bundle over to Sabbath Hawks, Haze's girlfriend. In a very humorous scene, she begins to rock the dead dwarf in her arms like a baby, telling Hazel, "Call me Momma now."[199]

> "Ask your daddy yonder where he was running off to—sick as he is?" Sabbath said. "Ask him isn't he going to take you and me with him?"
>
> The hand [Hazel's hand] that had been arrested in the air moved forward and plucked at the squinting face but without touching it; it reached again, slowly, and plucked at nothing and then it lunged and snatched the shriveled body and threw it against the wall. The head popped and the trash inside sprayed out in a little cloud of dust.[200]

This scene is a turning point in the novel because the Church Without Christ and the new jesus that Haze has been preaching are now in his midst. Enoch's gift is not an idea or a thought, but represents symbolically a kind of incarnation of the new god of modernity, and Haze, when confronted with this symbolic vision, outright rejects it. Bieber Lake observes:

> O'Connor has Enoch bring a dead body to Haze because it will activate Haze's wise blood. Although Haze wants to believe the modern view he teaches in his church that "the dead are dead and stay that way," he can find no power in the doctrine to ameliorate his fear of death. Modernity's scientific view can only work to put off death or separate us from it as long as possible—it cannot prepare us for it.... Haze must experience, with his senses, an actual dead body to remember that, for an atheist, real death is the necessary and indisputable end of men. Haze must feel the power of literal death in his gut before a literally resurrected Christ can mean anything.[201]

O'Connor was well aware of modernity's attempt to disregard mystery and to embrace a more mathematic or scientific approach to the world, even regarding problems that are not mathematic or scientific in nature. She uses Enoch Emery to address this disregard for mystery, first by showing his de-evolution from man into animal and then by his action of presenting Haze with an incarnation of the new jesus—a stolen, shriveled-up mummy. Both accounts of Enoch's actions are as humorous as they are horrifying, and both expose the consequences of modernity's disregard for mystery in a narrative only O'Connor could devise.

Knowing Through the Concreteness of Nature and Creation

In *Wise Blood* there is no one character who embodies the modern, rational, highly educated scientism or skepticism that we find in so many of O'Connor's other stories.[202] Yet there remains a strong critique of modernity's tendency to distrust the natural, created, concrete world and its ability to tell us anything about itself. The spiritualism and Gnosticism on display in *Wise Blood* is exposed not so much by the direct actions of characters, but by the observations and commentary of the narrator about the characters or about nature. We will examine a few examples below. The third chapter of *Wise Blood* begins with these words:

> His second night in Taulkinham, Hazel Motes walked along downtown close to the store fronts but not looking in them. The black sky was underpinned with long silver streaks that looked like scaffolding and depth on depth behind it were thousands of stars that all seemed to be moving very slowly as if they were about some vast construction work that involved the whole order of the universe and would take all time to complete. No one was paying any attention to the sky.[203]

We recall that according to Aquinas, knowledge begins with the senses, and that seeing holds priority of the five senses. Yet we are told by the narrator that Hazel refuses to look at the store fronts and that no one in Taulkinham was paying any attention to the beautiful night sky. These details suggest that the characters are marked by a dysfunctional solipsism. The fallen human being can be turned in on himself, and characterized by distrust of concrete reality, its ability to present truth, and our ability to know it as human beings. According to Aristotle, philosophy begins with wonder, and human beings, by their nature, want to know about reality.[204] This wonder is triggered by our relation to and interaction with the concrete world; it does not begin by denying our senses as we see in Descartes's *dubito*.

The reference to "depth on depth" is O'Connor's way of speaking to mystery, but we note that such mystery comes by way of contact with concrete reality and not apart from it. Human beings, through their interaction with and contemplation of the concrete world, enter into depths of reality and mystery that cannot be reached except through the concrete world. Cartesian inheritance, however, cuts the human person off from a deeper metaphysical engagement with the world of physical nature, and causes one to perceive nature only as a field of mechanics, no longer aware of its depth of being and riches of beauty that are symbolically expressive of the divine. The narrator of *Wise Blood* is informing the reader that the "stars that all seemed to be moving very slowly as if they were about some vast construction work that involved the whole order of the universe and would take all time to complete" do indeed have the power to tell human beings about themselves and even reveal something about the intelligence behind the stars, as well as the nature of the "vast construction work," but such knowledge is inaccessible if one refuses to look to and then trust the concrete world and our interaction with it as the starting point for knowledge.

In chapter 7, O'Connor uses the concrete, natural image of a cloud to symbolize the presence and providence of God in Hazel's life. In the second sentence of the chapter O'Connor writes, "The sky was just a little lighter blue than his suit, clear and even, with only one cloud in it, a large blinding white one with curls and a beard."[205] It is in this chapter that Haze is surprised to find Sabbath Lily Hawks hiding in his car during an afternoon drive through the country. Haze had planned to seduce Sabbath, but much of the chapter is about her attempts to seduce him. The cloud shows up again about halfway through the chapter:

> The blinding white cloud was a little ahead of them, moving to the left. "Why don't you turn down that dirt road?" she asked. The highway forked off onto a clay road and he turned onto it. It was hilly and shady and the country showed to advantage on either side. One side was dense honeysuckle and the other was open and slanted down to a telescoped view of the city. The white cloud was directly in front of them.[206]

One way to read this chapter is to consider that in order for Haze to turn away from his egocentric, self-obsessed ways, only a serious moral transgression—in this case, having illicit sexual relations with Sabbath—will afford him the possibility of conversion. The cloud then can be seen as God's presence, calling him back to Himself, even if that summons is caught up with a free act of fornication.[207] This is not to say that O'Connor thinks God is calling Haze to sin, but that Haze is so far from where he ought to be that it is only through a grave sin that he will realize how far he has fallen and then turn back to God.

Ultimately, although Hazel has the perfect opportunity, and although Sabbath Lily Hawks is willing and ready, they refrain from any carnal acts and the chapter ends with these two lines: "Haze drove on. The blinding white cloud had turned into a bird with long thin wings and was disappearing in the opposite direction."[208] The three references to the blinding white cloud in chapter 7 are significant not simply of God, but more specifically of the three persons of the Holy Trinity, as the first reference describes the cloud with a beard (God the Father), the second reference describes the cloud as directly in front of them (God the Son), and the third reference describes the cloud as a bird with long thin wings (God the Holy Spirit).

Unlike Descartes, who discovered his rational proofs for God's existence by turning away from the world and into his own mind, O'Connor uses the concrete reality of a cloud in the seventh chapter of *Wise Blood* not as a rational proof of God's existence, but to show her reader that human beings come to know God and his presence and providence through creation, that is, through the natural, concrete world and our contemplation of it.

Hazel Motes as Contemplative Monk

Unlike Enoch Emery, who regresses from human to animal,

Hazel Motes converts from grievous sinner into a model of sanctity, but his transformation comes at a grave cost—his life. For the majority of *Wise Blood,* Haze is running from God, rejecting the divine at every turn, even to the extreme of starting his own church and preaching a new jesus. If he worships anything beside himself and the Church Without Christ, it is his Essex automobile, a "high rat-colored" car that he purchases for forty dollars because he woke up one morning thinking "he was going to buy a car. The thought was full grown in his head when he woke up, and he didn't think of anything else. He had never thought before of buying a car; he had never even wanted one before. He had driven one only a little in his life and he didn't have any license."[209]

The rat-colored car is symbolic both of *technology* and *death.* It symbolizes technology because the Essex affords Haze modernity's dream: the freedom to go anywhere, without limits, to make his own path in life. "This car'll get me anywhere I want to go. It may stop here and there but it won't stop permanent."[210] Haze sees the rat-colored car as his salvation, exclaiming, "Nobody with a good car needs to be justified,"[211] which is one of the more humorous and revealing lines in the novel, because the car is a jalopy and the fact that Haze cannot see that truth points to his blurry vision of reality. The Essex symbolizes death because this car becomes the church and pulpit from which Haze preaches the Church Without Christ and proclaims the new jesus to whomever will listen, which, as we have shown above, is the gospel of death, a life apart from God that is symbolized by a corpse. The car is also the instrument Haze uses to kill a man.

Haze and his Essex are heading in the wrong direction, away from God and toward death, and so he needs to be turned around; he literally needs to be converted (*conversio*). As is typical of O'Connor, she uses three violent acts to bring about his full conversion. Before examining these three acts, we will look to O'Connor to explain why such violence is necessary:

> I have found that violence is strangely capable of returning my characters to reality and preparing them to accept their moment of grace. Their heads are so hard that almost nothing else will do the work. This idea, that reality is something to which we must be returned at considerable cost, is one which is seldom understood by the casual reader, but it is one which is implicit in the Christian view of the world.[212]

The first violent act that sets Haze's conversion in motion is his murder of Solace Layfield, a prophet and preacher of the Holy Church of Christ Without Christ, whose partner is Hoover Shoats. Shoats and Layfield have established a rival church to Haze's Church Without Christ and Haze sees them as a threat to his congregation. One night, after Shoats and Layfield clear fifteen dollars and thirty-five cents preaching their new gospel, Haze follows them in his car, and after watching Layfield drop off Shoats at his home, he chases Layfield down in his Essex. Now outside of town, Haze rams his Essex into the back of Layfield's car, prompting the "True Prophet" to get out and approach Haze, who is still in his Essex. Haze runs Layfield over, and then puts the car in reverse and runs him over again. Layfield attempts to make a confession before he dies, but Haze tells him to "shut up," though curiously he leans in closer to listen.

> The man was trying to say something but he was only wheezing. Haze squatted down by his face to listen. "Give my mother a lot of trouble," he said through a kind of bubbling in his throat. "Never giver no rest. Stole theter car. Never told the truth to my daddy or give Henry what, never give him . . ."
> "You shut up," Haze said, leaning his head closer to hear the confession.
> "Told where his still was and got five dollars for it," the man gasped.
> "You shut up now," Haze said.
> "Jesus . . ." the man said.
> "Shut up like I told you to now," Haze said.
> "Jesus hep me," the man wheezed.
> Haze gave him a hard slap on the back and he was quiet.[213]

In this scene the Essex becomes what it symbolizes, as Haze uses his high rat-colored car to inflict death upon another human being through an act of murder. On one hand this is the high point of Haze's anti-Gospel mission, as he has now incarnated his unholy word. Driving back to the city to continue preaching the Church Without Christ and the new jesus, Haze is filled with a new confidence in himself and in his Essex, stating, "this car is just beginning its life. A lightning bolt couldn't stop it."[214] But he soon finds himself pulled over by a patrolman, who asks for his license. When Haze fails to produce one for the officer, the second act of violence ensues:

> "Listen," the patrolman said, taking another tone, "would you mind driving your car up to the top of the next hill? I want you to see the view from up there, puttiest view you ever did see."
>
> Haze shrugged but he started the car up. He didn't mind fighting the patrolman if that was what he wanted. He drove to the top of the hill, with the patrol car following close behind him. "Now you turn it facing the embankment," the patrolman said. "You'll be able to see better thataway." Haze turned it facing the embankment. "Now maybe you better had get out," the cop said. "I think you could see better if you was out."
>
> Haze got out and glanced at the view. The embankment dropped down for about thirty feet, sheer washed-out red clay, into a partly burnt pasture where there was one scrub cow lying near a puddle. Over in the middle distance there was a one-room shack with a buzzard standing hunch-shouldered on the roof.
>
> The patrolman got behind the Essex and pushed it over the embankment and the cow stumbled up and galloped across the field and into the woods; the buzzard flapped off to a tree at the edge of the

clearing. The car landed on its top, with the three wheels that stayed on, spinning. The motor bounced out and rolled some distance away and various odd pieces scattered this way and that.

"Them that don't have a car, don't need a license," the patrolman said, dusting his hands on his pants.[215]

Haze had thought the Essex was his salvation, and that because of it, he did not need to be justified. The high rat-colored car symbolized his freedom, his mission, his philosophy, his theology, and his life. But the patrolman's violent act of pushing the car over the cliff and down the embankment leaves him with nothing; ironically, the anti-gospel that he has been preaching all along has now been delivered to him.

Seeing that the Church Without Christ and the new jesus have failed him, Haze's life takes a drastic turn in a new direction. His walk back to the city takes him three hours. We are told that Haze "stopped at a supply store and bought a tin bucket and a sack of quicklime and then he went on to where he lived, carrying these."[216] Once he arrives back home, his landlady, Mrs. Flood, notices him pouring lime into the bucket and then filling it with water. When she asks him what he plans on doing, he replies, "Blind myself," and then he does just that.

Hazel's violent act of blinding himself with lime is his acceptance of a new way of being, of a life of contemplation.[217] For the remainder of the novel, Haze becomes monk-like,[218] embracing a life of asceticism, practicing what are traditionally known as the evangelical counsels of poverty,[219] chastity,[220] and obedience.[221] His severe actions confound Mrs. Flood,[222] who Henry Edmondson argues "represents all those in need of 'The Flood' of Genesis. . . . [T]his woman stands for all those in need of judgment and redemption—the entire human race."[223]

We recall that the final chapter of Guardini's *The Spirit of the Liturgy* is entitled "The Primacy of the Logos," and his commentary on contemplative religious orders in this chapter offers an important insight into Hazel Motes's mortification. Guardini writes:

> This predominance of the will and the idea of its value gives the present day its peculiar character. It is the reason for its restless pressing forward, the stringent limiting of its hours of labor, the precipitancy of its enjoyment; hence, too, the worship of success, of strength, of action; hence the striving after power, and generally the exaggerated opinion of the value of time, and the compulsion to exhaust oneself by activity till the end. This is the reason, too, why spiritual organizations such as the old contemplative orders, which formerly were automatically accepted by spiritual life everywhere and which were the darlings of the orthodox world, are not infrequently misunderstood even by Catholics, and have to be defended by their friends against the reproach of idle trifling. . . . The practical will is everywhere the decisive factor, and the Ethos has complete

precedence over the Logos, the active side of life over the contemplative.[224]

In Haze's action of self-blinding and then his embrace of the contemplative life, O'Connor reclaims the medieval priority of *Logos* over *Ethos* and contemplation over action. O'Connor is certainly familiar with those who criticize men and women in contemplative religious orders for not "doing anything" with their lives, but Edmondson argues that O'Connor is working out a distinction between the modern notion of leisure as passive entertainment and the medieval idea of leisure as personal improvement.[225] Edmondson observes, "Engagement in leisure, in the classical sense, may at times look like idleness. Because [Haze] rarely speaks, Mrs. Flood is often annoyed at him. He mystifies her."[226] O'Connor, then, is out to show her reader that the highest form of living is not one driven by emotions, or actions, or the will, but the intellect in contemplation. However, this sort of life is often misconstrued, so Bieber Lake makes an important clarification:

> Finally, while self-blinding and self-mortification may seem to be a turn away from the physical world, it can actually be a turn toward it. Critics note that when Haze blinds himself, he does so as a medieval ascetic might: he repudiates the physical world in favor of the spiritual. But ascetics are not necessarily Gnostics. Medieval asceticism in particular acknowledges the body's essential and inescapable role in our spiritual lives at the same time it acknowledges that the body

tries always to claim undue absolute sovereignty. In short, ascetics know better than anyone how important the body is.[227]

Haze's act of self-blinding and his turn to the contemplative life is not so much an outright rejection of his emotions, his actions, or his will, as it is a prioritization of his life by bringing discipline to those areas that threaten to overrule his intellect and keep him from a life of contemplation and serenity.[228] In this way Hazel Motes becomes the "pin point of light"[229] that invites the reader of *Wise Blood* to follow his example.

Conclusion

In Caroline Gordon's reckoning, Flannery O'Connor's picture of the modern world is "literally terrifying." The good news is that O'Connor's vision of reality is ultimately one of joyful hope, not terrifying despair. However, in order to bring her readers to this final end, O'Connor finds it necessary to address four "knots" of modernity: the self as the center of existence; a disregard for mystery; a general distrust of the concrete; and the subordination of reason.

While I was practicing for our annual priests vs. seminarians basketball game recently at one of our grade school gyms in the Diocese of Cleveland, I was struck by the glossy banners of individual child athletes that decorated the walls of the gymnasium. The kind of décor that once was limited to an NBA arena with the names and images of star players has made its way down to childhood sports. Everyone has his or her own poster; each boy or girl is somehow a star. This is not to say that young people don't need affirmation and encouragement—they certainly do—but it is to say that our culture places a tremendous amount of emphasis on the self, presenting "unique selfhood" as an achievement that deserves constant celebration. Consider how social media pressures us to focus on ourselves, to establish a brand, and to curate our life experiences to impress and influence others. It's all a part of that first knot that O'Connor noticed—the self as center of existence. For O'Connor, God is the center of existence, and we find our true selves when we find ourselves in him. History and self-reflection teach us that it is in human nature to always worship something, and if we don't worship God then we are liable to worship ourselves. O'Connor's fiction reveals the range of ways in which we can remake reality in our own image, idolatrously elevating our own importance until–often unknowingly–we've placed ourselves on the seat that belongs to God alone. O'Connor aims to shock us out of this self-absorption.

    Flannery O'Connor died a year before the closing of the Second Vatican Council, so she would have worn some sort of head covering while participating in Mass and devotions, as was the custom for Catholic women of her day. (See the biopic *Wildcat* starring Maya Hawke for an embodiment of this practice.) Although head covering is no longer mandated, some young Catholic women are opting to "veil" in church, a practice which comforts some and frustrates others. While this essay is not the place to discuss the issue of veiling at Mass, what the veil stands for, and what veiling signifies, biblically speaking, is of great significance. A veil protects mystery; it is a sign of reverence for something holy. O'Connor was concerned that all too often people consider God a math problem or a puzzle to be solved, rather than as the all-mysterious One who solves us. Something similar is true of human beings created in God's image and likeness. We are more than our blood type, our height or weight, our salary, our neighborhood, our job, our Myers-Briggs letters, or anything that can be measured. The second knot of modernity for O'Connor is treating God and human persons as data points to be used and manipulated rather than as mysteries to be contemplated and loved. Her fiction is constantly working to bring her reader back to the mysteries of God, of ourselves, and all of Creation.

O'Connor would not be surprised to hear people in 2025 say, "I'm spiritual, not religious." Religion is specific and concrete, particularly the Catholic kind with the Triune God and the Incarnation; the Magisterium and the Bible; the Blessed Mother and Saints; the ten commandments and the seven sacraments; baptismal gowns and religious garb; doctrines and dogma; male and female bodies; nativity scenes and stations of the cross; relics and shrines; corporal and spiritual works of mercy; devotions and novenas—all specific, all concrete. O'Connor submitted to this path from particularity to mystery. But she also saw that the third knot of modernity condemns these specific and concrete things as *too* specific and *too* concrete; for the modern, autonomous self, they are too demanding and too restrictive of the human person. And, therefore, the "spiritual person" may find it more liberating to embrace a gnostic belief, a practice with more wiggle room and idealized–often abstract–principles. But O'Connor believes in specificity, so for her, although we humans are spiritual beings, we are also material ones. Matter matters. Things matter. The concrete realities of day-to-day living matter. Human action matters. Through a variety of characters who favor ideology over reality —Hulga, Rayber, Asbury, Julian, to name just a few—O'Connor reveals that such spiritual liberties and disembodied abstractions will culminate in frustration and loneliness rather than the promised liberation the human heart desires.

The final knot of modernity, according to O'Connor, is perhaps the most pernicious and most ubiquitous of all—the subordination of reason. We human beings are like other animals in that we move, feel, reproduce, and have natural appetites. Yet we are unlike other animals in our powers of intellect and will, that is, in our ability to know what is good or bad, true or false, beautiful or ugly, and our ability to choose one over the other. We are also unlike other animals in our ability to love, which is not simply an emotion, feeling, or passion, but an act of the will: "There is no greater love than this: to lay down one's life for one's friends" (John 15:13). Love is an act; it is something we choose to do. Sometimes it feels great, other times it is excruciatingly painful, yet it is never just a feeling or an emotion or a passion. However, some of the most common mantras of our day are: "follow your heart," "follow your dreams," and "follow your passion," which at first glance seem like innocuous phrases. However, when we truly test them on the level of reality, their allure proves hollow, their consequences grave. A man has made a marriage vow to his wife. They have three children together. A decade into their marriage, he falls in love with another woman, a woman who makes his heart swell, who promises fulfillment of the dreams he discarded when he took a job to support his children. Who, looking soberly at the situation, could without qualms counsel the man to follow his heart and leave his wife for the new woman? Love keeps its promises, especially when it hurts. That's why married couples make vows in the first place. Most couples don't "need" the vows on their wedding day, but they will need them down the road when times aren't good, or someone gets sick, or when someone "falls out of love." In Plato's *Republic*, the virtuous city/soul is the one where the rational faculty rules the appetites with the help of the emotions. The vicious city/soul, on the contrary, arises when reason has been subjugated by the passions. Flannery O'Connor is certainly not a Stoic, and she had a great capacity for deep and authentic love, yet she did believe that real love was far more than romance, sentimental affections, or tenderness, far more than the professional compassion of the therapeutic. For O'Connor, real love was identified by the willingness to sacrifice for the sake of the other, which often requires one to go against one's emotions and desires for the sake of the good. The title of her second novel, *The Violent Bear It Away* (Matthew 11:12), puts it powerfully.

I hope, dear reader, that you now have a better understanding of some of the problems of modernity, of the knots that snarl your life, yet perhaps haven't been able to name. I hope that burdens particular to our times have been lightened by these insights. For all her fame, many find Flannery O'Connor's art more weird than wonderful. I hope, dear reader, that you close this little book understanding the *why* of her weirdness, and why, too, she never left the Church. When that strangeness "can be sensed as a figure for our essential displacement," I reckon all of us might just be ready to be redeemed.

Endnotes

1. Caroline Gordon, "May 15 Is Publication Date of Novel by Flannery O'Connor, Milledgeville," in *Conversations with Flannery O'Connor* (Jackson: University Press of Mississippi, 1987), 3.

2. I treat O'Connor's Hillbilly Thomism extensively in my previous book: Damian Ference, *Understanding the Hillbilly Thomist: The Philosophical Foundations of Flannery O'Connor's Narrative Art* (Elk Grove Village, IL: Word on Fire, 2023).

3. O'Connor was grateful for her doctor (whom she called "The Scientist") and modern medicine in general, as well as for her electric typewriter and the ice crusher—still attached to the kitchen wall at Andalusia to this day—which made it easier for her to prepare martinis.

4. Paul Elie, *The Life You Save May Be Your Own: An American Pilgrimage* (New York: Farrar, Straus and Giroux, 2003), 270.

5. Cf. John 17:14–16; Romans 12:2.

6. Brad Gooch, *Flannery: A Life of Flannery O'Connor* (New York: Little, Brown and Company, 2009), 113–14.

7. "He studied in Tübingen (1903–04; 1906–08), Munich (1904–05), Berlin (1905–06) and Freiburg (1906)." Holger Zaborowski, "Contradiction, Liturgy, and Freedom: Romano Guardini's Search for Meaning After the Cataclysm of World War I," *Modern Theology* 35:1 (January 2019): 45.

8. Zaborowski, "Contradiction," 44.

9. Christopher Shannon, "Romano Guardini: Father of the New Evangelization," Crisis Magazine, February 17, 2014, accessed November 20, 2019, https://www.crisismagazine.com/2014/romano-guardini-father-of-the-new-evangelization

10. Zaborowski, "Contradiction," 46.

11. "While neo-scholasticism declared eternal truths with no significant reference to their historical context and with

no sensitivity for the historically concrete and particular situation, Guardini's thought is deeply historical." Zaborowski, "Contradiction," 46.

12 "Guardini abandoned any kind of thought that put abstract principles and formalistic rationality at its center." Zaborowski, "Contradiction," 46.

13 Shannon, "Guardini."

14 Shannon, "Guardini."

15 Romano Guardini, *The Conversion of Augustine*, trans. Elinor Briefs (London: Sands and Company Publishers, 1960), xvii.

16 ST I, q. 84, a. 1.

17 By "overly rationalistic" here I mean an emphasis on logical forms of argument to the detriment of reflection on personal experience.

18 Christopher Shannon notes: "He did not speak the language of Thomism and generally avoided the axe-grinding, triumphalist apologetics that were the stuff of mainstream Catholic 'engagement' with the world. His lectures did, however, attract some of the brightest young minds of his day, including Josef Pieper, Hans Urs von Balthasar, and Hannah Arendt. In reaching out to the world, Guardini looked for theological themes in places where Thomists feared to tread—namely modern literature and Eastern religions. In these explorations, Guardini often found himself perceived as too 'liberal' for mainstream Catholics and too Catholic for mainstream secularists." Shannon, "Guardini."

19 See the final chapter of *The Spirit of the Liturgy*, entitled "The Primacy of Logos Over Ethos." Romano Guardini, *The Spirit of the Liturgy*, trans. Ada Lane (New York: The Crossroad Publishing Company, 1997).

20 Some nuance is in order regarding this claim that Guardini was drawn to Augustine's *existential* philosophy. It is true that as a philosophical movement existentialism is most often associated with post-war European thinkers such as Sartre, Camus, and de Beauvoir as a philosophy that insists that *existence precedes essence*. In this regard Augustine is not an existentialist in the strict sense, for as Gordon Lewis has argued, "The fundamental banner under which all existentialists fly is intended to deny the

very thing Augustine asserts. Augustine defends his identification of the Platonic ideas with the mind of God..." Gordon R. Lewis, "Augustine and Existentialism," *Bulletin of the Evangelical Theological Society*, no. 8 (Winter 1965): 17. However, Augustine can be said to be existential in style, point of view, and attitude in a way that could not be said of Thomas, most famously on display in his *Confessions*. For as Lewis notes, "Augustine's account of his own experience seems to indicate [an existentialist] point of view. His *Confessions* express the incessant restlessness of the individual separated from God. He sought pleasure, honor, and truth, not in God the Creator, but in creatures. His childhood was filled with temper tantrums, pride, inexcusable jealousies, lies and lust. Mentally as well as morally he was restless. Like a character from a modern novel Augustine at the age of thirty was filled with increasing anxiety, a silent trembling, a loathing of self, an internal war" (Lewis, 14). So Augustine was not an existentialist in the strict sense, since he believed in God and universals, but with Lewis we can say with confidence that "Augustine has an existentialist standpoint of human fallenness, an emphasis on the existing individual, and an existential attitude of involvement" (Lewis, 22). Guardini himself writes, "Augustinian thought tends to the existential, the word taken in its strictest (Kierkegaardian) sense.... But again and again he transcends this form of thought, passing on to that in which the thinker, one with all existence, co-experiences it and actively participating in its fulfillment by his thought, attempts to grasp existence as a whole." Guardini, *Augustine*, 70.

[21] Flannery O'Connor, *The Habit of Being: Letters of Flannery O'Connor*. Edited by Sally Fitzgerald (New York, Farrar, Straus and Giroux, 1979), 74.

[22] 1. *The Death of Socrates: An Interpretation of the Platonic Dialogues: Euthyphro, Apology, Crito and Phaedo*, trans. B. Jowett (New York: Walter J. Black, 1942); 2. *The Faith and Modern Man*, trans. Charlotte E. Forsyth (New York: Pantheon, 1952); 3. *Jesus Christus: Meditations*, trans. Peter White (Chicago: Henry Regnery, 1959); 4. *The Lord*, trans. Elinor Castendyk (Chicago: Henry Regnery, 1954); 5. *Freedom, Grace, and Destiny: Three Chapters in the Interpretation of Existence*, trans. John Murray, S.J. (New York: Pantheon, 1961); 6. *The Conversion of Augustine*,

trans. Elinor Briefs (Westminster, MD: Newman Press, 1960); 7. *The Rosary of Our Lady*, trans. H. von Schuecking (New York: P.J. Kennedy and Sons, 1955); 8. *Meditations Before Mass*, trans. Elinor Castendyk Briefs (Westminster, MD: Newman Press, 1956); 9. *Prayer in Practice*, trans. Prince Leopold of Loewenstein-Wertheim (New York: Pantheon: 1957); 10. *Prayers from Theology*, trans. Richard Newnham (New York: Herder and Herder, 1959); *Sacred Signs*, trans. Grace Branham (St. Louis, Mo: Pio Decimo Press: 1956).

[23] Flannery O'Connor, *The Presence of Grace and Other Book Reviews by Flannery O'Connor*. Edited by Carter W. Martin (Athens, GA: The University of Georgia Press, 1983). 1. *The Rosary of Our Lady* (*Presence of Grace*, 16–17); 2. *Meditations Before Mass* (*Presence of Grace*, 28); 3. *Prayer in Practice* (*Presence of Grace*, 52–53); 4. *Jesus Christus* (*Presence of Grace*, 85); 5. *The Conversion of Augustine* (*Presence of Grace*, 113–14); 6. *Freedom, Grace, and Destiny* (*Presence of Grace*, 123).

[24] Guardini was born in Verona, Italy, but his family moved to Mainz, Germany, a year later. Zaborowski, "Contradiction," 45.

[25] O'Connor, *Presence of Grace*, 28.

[26] O'Connor, *Presence of Grace*, 16–17.

[27] It is a most Thomistic move on O'Connor's part to recognize truth where she finds it, even if that truth comes to her from the Augustinian tradition.

[28] O'Connor, *Habit of Being*, 104.

[29] O'Connor, *Habit of Being*, 169.

[30] O'Connor, *Presence of Grace*, 17.

[31] O'Connor, *Presence of Grace*, 53.

[32] O'Connor, *Habit of Being*, 92.

[33] Cf. Romano Guardini, *The End of the Modern World* (Wilmington, DE: Intercollegiate Studies Institute, 2001). This title is not part of O'Connor's library and it is not clear that she ever read it; however, this work does present the philosophical theme of man's alienation, the context against which Guardini's entire canon may be read. In his review of this work, Wayne Allen notes, "This forms

the backdrop of Guardini's thesis: Modernity has disconnected man from his history and uprooted him from a 'place' in the world. The significance of place is twofold: It means the experiential reality located in past human events, and an orientation for man's actions within a cosmology that preceded him and of which he is a part." Wayne Allen, "Romano Guardini and the Dissolution of Western Culture," *The Imaginative Conservative* (May 8, 2013), accessed February 27, 2020, https://theimaginativeconservative.org/2017/08/romano-guardini-dissolution-western-culture-wayne-allen-timeless.html

[34] Charles Taylor, *A Secular Age* (Cambridge: The Belknap Press of Harvard University Press, 2007), 25.

[35] Guardini notes, "From the standpoint of understanding of critical methodology, Augustine thinks neither 'philosophically' nor 'theologically.' His thought does contain a philosophy as well as a theology, but both are hidden. Anyone wishing to examine them must first dig them out, and this is no easy excavation. Many unfortunate misunderstandings would have been avoided had this fact been faced more squarely, and had fewer attempts been made to employ Augustinian thought like Thomistic, or even like that of a nineteenth century theologian. Augustinian thought is of the period before the split into philosophy and theology. It is a Christian reflection; it is the reflections of a Christian man on existence – not on abstract existence, but on very real: existence as determined by God." Guardini, *Augustine*, 69.

[36] Guardini, *Augustine*, 69.

[37] O'Connor, *Presence of Grace*, 28.

[38] O'Connor is interested in distortion, which is a type of exaggeration, but different from the kind of exaggeration Guardini has in mind here.

[39] The *Ave Maria* was a Catholic magazine, popular in O'Connor's day, that Lynch had called "the worst magazine in the Catholic Press." O'Connor, *Habit of Being*, 173.

[40] O'Connor, *Habit of Being*, 139.

[41] See O'Connor's letter to Janet McKane (*Habit of Being*, 582) or almost any page of her *Prayer Journal* for evidence of her Marian devotion.

42 O'Connor, *Presence of Grace*, 52-53.

43 O'Connor, *Presence of Grace*, 52-53.

44 O'Connor, *Habit of Being*, 370.

45 Shannon, "Guardini."

46 Joseph Ratzinger, "Introduction," in Romano Guardini, *The Lord*, trans. Elinor Castendyk Briefs (Washington, DC: Gateway Publishing, 1996), xii.

47 O'Connor, *Habit of Being*, 93.

48 O'Connor, *Habit of Being*, 572.

49 "Étienne Gilson was born in Paris in 1884. He became professor of medieval philosophy at the Sorbonne in 1921, and from 1932 until his retirement in 1951 he held a similar chair at the College de France. From 1929 until his death in 1978 he was associated with the Pontifical Institute of Medieval Studies at the University of Toronto." From the back cover of Étienne Gilson, *The Christian Philosophy of St. Thomas Aquinas*, trans. L.K. Shook (Notre Dame: University of Notre Dame Press, 1994).

50 Étienne Gilson, *The Spirit of Medieval Philosophy*, trans. A.H.C. Downs (Notre Dame: University of Notre Dame, 1991), 6.

51 Cf. John F. Wippel, *The Metaphysical Thought of Thomas Aquinas: From Finite Being to Uncreated Being* (Washington, DC: The Catholic University of America Press, 2000), xvii.

52 Gilson, *Christian Philosophy*, viii.

53 "I am currently reading Étienne Gilson's *History of Christian Philosophy in the Middle Ages...*" *Habit of Being*, 107; "I have just read a large book called *Art and Reality* by [Étienne] Gilson and I don't believe the word emotion even came up in it." *Habit of Being*, 279. (No book exists by Gilson entitled "*Art and Reality*," so it is almost certain that O'Connor meant to write "*Painting and Reality*." It is also worth noting that on page 251 of *Painting and Reality* Gilson does mention the word *emotion*: "There is a genre of emotion that is entirely peculiar to painting: nothing else gives an idea of it.")

54 O'Connor, *Habit of Being*, 107.

55 Desmond J. FitzGerald, Foreword to Étienne Gilson, *The Unity of*

Philosophical Experience (San Francisco: Ignatius Press, 1999), ix.

56   Gilson, *Unity* x–xi.

57   Gilson, *Unity*, 255.

58   For example, consider the tension between the characters of Tarwater and Rayber in *VBA*, where Rayber is constantly depicted as "living in his head" while both Old and Young Tarwater are shown as being able to act, each living in the world and not lost in his own consciousness.

59   O'Connor, *Habit of Being*, 231.

60   O'Connor, *Habit of Being*, 477.

61   O'Connor, *Presence of Grace*, 129.

62   O'Connor, *Habit of Being*, 494.

63   Étienne Gilson, *Painting and Reality* (New York: Pantheon Books, 1957), x.

64   Gilson, *Painting*, xi.

65   O'Connor, *Presence of Grace*, 57.

66   Gilson, *Painting*, 258.

67   Flannery O'Connor, *Mystery and Manners: Occasional Prose*. Edited by Sally and Robert Fitzgerald (New York: Farrar, Straus and Giroux, 1969), 31.

68   Gilson, *Painting*, 293.

69   Gilson, *Painting*, 294.

70   O'Connor, *Habit of Being*, 92.

71   Gooch, *A Life*, 113.

72   Cf. part two: THE CARTESIAN EXPERIMENT; Chapter V. Cartesian Mathematicism; Chapter VI. Cartesian Spiritualism; Chapter VII. Cartesian Idealism; Chapter VIII. The Breakdown of Cartesianism.

73   Gilson, *Unity*, 143–44.

74   Gilson, *Unity*, 313.

75   Gilson, *Unity*, 226.

76 Guardini, *Augustine*, 32–33.
77 O'Connor, *Mystery and Manners*, 159.
78 O'Connor, *Habit of Being*, 302-03.
79 O'Connor, *Mystery and Manners*, 153.
80 Gabriel Marcel, *The Mystery of Being: I. Reflection and Mystery* (Chicago: Henry Regnery Company, 1950).
81 O'Connor, *Habit of Being*, 296.
82 O'Connor, *Habit of Being*, 463.
83 O'Connor, *Habit of Being*, 297.
84 Marcel, *Mystery*, 218.
85 Marcel, *Mystery*, 219.
86 Marcel, *Mystery*, 212.
87 Cf. Timothy J. Basselin, *Flannery O'Connor: Writing a Theology of Disabled Humanity* (Waco: Baylor University Press, 2013).
88 Marcel, *Mystery*, 209.
89 In the following sections I am interpreting Descartes primarily through Gilson, as it was Gilson's interpretation of Descartes that most influenced O'Connor, as we have seen above.
90 René Descartes, *Discourse on Method*, in *Selected Philosophical Writings*, trans. John Cottingham, Robert Stoothoff, and Dugald Murdoch (New York: Cambridge University Press, 1988), 7.
91 Descartes, *Discourse*, 8.
92 Gilson, *Unity*, 99.
93 Aristotle makes these distinctions in Book Six of the *Nicomachean Ethics* (1138b–1145a12) and Michael Allen Gillespie offers a succinct summary of this section in *The Theological Origins of Modernity* (Chicago: The University of Chicago Press, 2008), 186–87. He notes, "Practical knowledge is of two sorts, the knowledge of things made (*techne*), and the knowledge of things done (*phronesis*). Theoretical knowledge involves the knowledge of first principles (*nous*) and deduction from these first principles (*episteme*), which together constitute wisdom (*sophia*)."

94 Descartes, *Discourse*, 19.
95 Gilson, *Unity*, 111.
96 Gillespie, *Origins*, 187.
97 Gilson, *Unity*, 113.
98 Charles Taylor, *Secular Age*, 284.
99 Flannery O'Connor, *The Complete Stories* (New York: Farrar, Straus and Giroux, 1971), 268.
100 O'Connor, *Complete Stories*, 268–269.
101 O'Connor, *Complete Stories*, 270.
102 Scientism: "the belief that the methods of natural science, or the categories and things recognized in natural science, form the only proper elements in any philosophical or other inquiry." Simon Blackburn, "Scientism," *The Oxford Dictionary of Philosophy* (Oxford: Oxford University Press, 2005), 331. Gilson also notes that "paving the way to a purely mechanical physics, biology and medicine was the thing in which [Descartes] was most interested, and this may perhaps account for his readiness in asking metaphysics to pay the price for it." Gilson, *Unity*, 128.
103 Descartes, *Discourse,* 17.
104 In Meditation 3, Descartes offers his proof for God's existence known as *the craftsman stamp* (52) and in Meditation 5 he offers his ontological argument for God's existence (66–70).
105 Gilson, *Unity*, 162–163.
106 Gillespie, *Origins*, 190.
107 Descartes, *Discourse*, 62.
108 Richard Kennington, *On Modern Origins: Essays in Early Modern Philosophy* (New York: Lexington Books, 2004), 137.
109 Gilson, *Unity*, 128.
110 Taylor, *Secular Age*, 348.
111 Del Noce notes, "in Descartes we have at the same time the experience of freedom, which is his religious theme, and a form of separatism which coincides, if we look carefully, with the very principle of immanence that later will be developed to such a large

extent in modern philosophy." Del Noce, *The Crisis of Modernity*, trans. Carlo Lancellotti (London: McGill-Queen's University Press, 2014), 15.

112 Taylor, *Secular Age*, 329.

113 Cf. Michael Hanby, "Augustine and Descartes: An Overlooked Chapter in the Story of Modern Origins" *Modern Theology* 19:4 (October 2003), 475.

114 Gilson, *Unity*, 149.

115 Gilson, *Unity*, 168.

116 Jonathan I. Israel, *Radical Enlightenment: Philosophy and the Making of Modernity* 1650–1750 (Oxford: Oxford University Press, 2001), vi.

117 Gilson, *Unity*, 168.

118 Frederick Copleston notes, "God possesses an infinity of attributes, each of which is infinite; and of these two are known to us, namely, thought and extension. Finite minds are modes of God under the attribute of thought, and finite bodies are modes of God under the attribute of extension. Nature is not ontologically distinct from God; and the reason why it cannot be ontologically distinct is that God is infinite. He must comprise himself in all reality." Frederick Copleston, *A History of Philosophy: Vol. 4 Modern Philosophy: Descartes to Leibniz* (New York: Image Books, 1963), 223.

119 Israel, *Radical Enlightenment*, 231.

120 Israel, *Radical Enlightenment*, 231.

121 Israel, *Radical Enlightenment*, 221.

122 Israel, *Radical Enlightenment*, 13.

123 O'Connor, *Mystery and Manners*, 175.

124 O'Connor, *Habit of Being*, 299–300.

125 Israel, *Radical Enlightenment*, 218.

126 Israel, *Radical Enlightenment*, 220.

127 Israel, *Radical Enlightenment*, 232.

128 O'Connor, *Habit of Being*, 479.

[129] O'Connor, *Habit of Being*, 489.

[130] Gilson, *Unity*, 122.

[131] Gilson, *Unity*, 121.

[132] Guardini, *Augustine*, 50.

[133] O'Connor, *Mystery and Manners*, 68.

[134] Thomas Aquinas, *Summa theologiae*. Edited by Anton C. Pegis (New York: Modern Library,1948), 1.84.6

[135] Gilson, *Unity*, 130.

[136] Guardini, *Augustine*, 50.

[137] O'Connor, *Mystery and Manners*, 91.

[138] O'Connor, *Mystery and Manners*, 90-91.

[139] O'Connnor, *Habit of Being*, 84.

[140] O'Connor, *Mystery and Manners*, 96.

[141] Guardini, *The Lord*, 481.

[142] O'Connor, *Mystery and Manners*, 203.

[143] Robert P. George, "Gnostic Liberalism" *First Things*, no. 268 (December 2016): 33–34.

[144] Timothy Basselin notes, "This mystery of grace-from-suffering, portrayed again and again in her fiction, resulted from the daily mercy that was her own sickness. To put it differently, O'Connor was a good woman because lupus was there every minute of her adult life. Lupus was her mercy, it was appropriate, because lupus fashioned the good within her." Basselin, *Disabled Humanity*, 3.

[145] "For moral sentimentalists, our emotions and desires play a leading role in the anatomy of morality. Some believe moral thoughts are fundamentally sentimental, others that moral facts make essential reference to our sentimental responses, or that emotions are the primary source of moral knowledge. Some believe all these things. The two main attractions of sentimentalism are making sense of the practical aspects of morality, on the one hand, and finding a place for morality within a naturalistic worldview, on the other." Antti Kauppinen, "Moral Sentimentalism," Stanford Encyclopedia of Philosophy (January

29, 2014), accessed March 12, 2020, https://plato.stanford.edu/entries/moral-sentimentalism/

[146] There are various forms of voluntarism, but what I mean here is primarily the priority of the will over the intellect in theology (Scotus), epistemology (Van Fraassen), and morality (Kant, Schopenhauer, Nietzsche).

[147] "But the difference which constitutes man is *rational*, which is said of man because of his intellectual principle." ST I, q. 76, a. 1.

[148] Angèle Kremer-Marietti, "Comte, Isidore-Auguste-Marie-François-Xavier (1798–1857)," *Routledge Encyclopedia of Philosophy*, trans. Mary Pickering (London: Routledge, 1998), 496.

[149] Michel Bourdeau "Auguste Comte", *The Stanford Encyclopedia of Philosophy* (Summer 2018 Edition), Edward N. Zalta (ed.), https://plato.stanford.edu/archives/sum2018/entries/comte/.

[150] Comte famously argues that each branch of human knowledge passes through three different theoretical states: 1. the theological or fictitious state; 2. the metaphysical or abstract state; and 3. the scientific or positive state, which leads to the *theological method*, the *metaphysical method*, and the *positive method*. Comte explains, "Hence, there are three kinds of philosophy or general systems or conceptions on the aggregate of phenomena which are mutually exclusive of each other. The first is the necessary starting point of human intelligence; the third represents its fixed and definitive state; the second is destined to serve only as a transitional method." Auguste Comte, *Introduction to Positive Philosophy*, trans. Frederick Ferré (Indianapolis: Hackett Publishing Company, 1988), 1–2. And in *A General View of Positivism*, Comte writes, "The subjective principle in Positivism, that is, the subordination of the intellect to the heart is thus fortified by an objective basis, the immutable Necessity of the external world; and by this means it becomes possible to bring human life within the influence of social sympathy." Auguste Comte, *A General View of Positivism: Chapters I and IV (abridged)* in *The European Philosophers: From Descartes to Nietzsche*, trans. J.H. Bridges (New York: The Modern Library, 1992) 739.

[151] Gilson, *Unity*, 212.

152 Gilson, *Unity,* 206.

153 Gilson, *Unity,* 246.

154 Gilson, *Unity,* 211.

155 Auguste Comte, *A General View of Positivism: Chapters I and IV* (abridged) in The European Philosophers: From Descartes to Nietzsche, trans. J.H. Bridges (New York: The Modern Library, 1992) 736.

156 Gilson, *Unity,* 212.

157 For an in-depth treatment on this topic, see Damian Ference, *Understanding the Hillbilly Thomist: The Philosophical Foundations of Flannery O'Connor's Narrative Art* (Elk Grove Village, IL: Word on Fire, 2023), chapter 4, "The Ethics of Flannery O'Connor."

158 Kremer-Marietti, "Comte," 501.

159 Gilson notes, "By thus making love the ultimate foundation of positivism, Comte was repeating, in his own way, and for reasons that were entirely his own, Kant's famous move decreeing the primacy of practical reason. Obviously Comte owed nothing to Kant, but, left as he was with the task of contriving a philosophy without metaphysics, he had no choice other than some sort of moralism. Comte's moralism was to be the sentimentalism which asserts itself at the beginning of his *Discours sur l'ensemble du Positivisme.*" Gilson, *Unity,* 211.

160 Romano Guardini, *The Spirit of the Liturgy,* trans. Ada Lane (New York: The Crossroads Publishing Company, 1998), 86-87.

161 For an account of the history of voluntarism see Servais Pinckaers, *The Sources of Christian Ethics,* trans. Mary Thomas Noble (Washington, D.C.: The Catholic University of America Press, 1995).

162 Romano Guardini, *The Spirit of the Liturgy,* 92.

163 Romano Guardini, *The Spirit of the Liturgy,* 88–89.

164 Romano Guardini, *The Spirit of the Liturgy,* 91.

165 Flannery O'Connor, *A Prayer Journal.* Edited by W.A. Sessions (New York: Farrar, Straus and Giroux, 2013), 5.

166 O'Connor, *Mystery and Manners,* 147–48.

167 O'Connor, *Habit of Being*, 99–100.

168 "Romanticism is a broad movement of thought in philosophy, the arts, history, and political theory, at its height in Germany, England and France towards the end of the 18th and in the earlier part of the 19th centuries. Romanticism can be defined as a reaction against the rationalism and empiricism of the period of the Enlightenment: romanticism is best characterized by its idealist celebration of the self, by its respect for the transcendental, and by its conviction of the power of the imagination and of the supreme value of art." Cf. "Romanticism: Philosophical Definition", *The-Philosophy.com*, accessed April 14, 2020, https://www.the-philosophy.com/romanticism-philosophical-definition.

169 O'Connor, *Mystery and Manners*, 227.

170 O'Connor mentions the relationship between *reason* and *feeling* three times in her *Prayer Journal*; we have already noted one instance above. Here are the other two: "It is the adoration of You, dear God, that most dismays me. I cannot comprehend the exaltation that must be due You. Intellectually, I assent: let us adore God. But can we do that without feeling? To feel, we must know." PJ, 8; and, "I have been reading Mr. Kafka and I feel his problem of getting grace. But I see it doesn't have to be that way for the Catholic who can go to communion every day. The Msgr. today said it was the business of reason, not emotion—the love of God. The emotion would be a help. I realized last time that it would be a selfish one. Oh dear God, the reason is very empty. I suppose mine is also lazy. But I want to get near You." PJ, 13.

171 Although I present O'Connor's four philosophical themes of modernity in this section according to particular characters, themes, and situations found in *Wise Blood*, it should be noted that these four themes of modernity run throughout the novella and cannot be pinned down in a clear and distinct manner to one specific instantiation.

172 Christina Bieber Lake, *The Incarnational Art of Flannery O'Connor* (Macon, GA: Mercer University Press, 2005), 57.

173 Flannery O'Connor, *Wise Blood* (New York: Farrar, Straus and Giroux, 1952), 21–21.

174 O'Connor, *Wise Blood*, 105.

175 A disciple of Auguste Comte, Henry Edger, literally founded a Comtean church, building an oratory and steeple next to his log cabin. Gillis Harp explains, "Accordingly, the Comtist church would have a full sacramental system that would infuse with sanctity and meaning various stages in the growth of an individual. These were presentation (corresponding to baptism), initiation (first communion?), admission (confirmation?), destination, marriage, maturity, retreat (retirement?) and even transformation (death). Edger also promoted the Comtean calendar patterned after the Catholic liturgical calendar that commemorated the lives of the saints. Comte's calendar sought to inject historical significance into each week and month of the year by naming them after great figures of religion, art, science or government." Gillis J. Harp, "The Church of Humanity: New York's Worshipping Positivists," *Church History* 60, no. 4 (December 4, 1991): 511.

176 O'Connor, *Wise Blood*, 148.

177 Guardini, *Augustine*, 124.

178 O'Connor, *Mystery and Manners*, 34.

179 Bieber Lake, *Incarnational Art*, 65.

180 Guardini, *Augustine*, 62–3.

181 Margaret Earley Whitt provides an excellent explanation of the meaning of this character's name. She notes that Enoch "shares his name with the biblical Enoch, one of two people from the Old Testament who was taken up into heaven without dying" and that "the biblical Enoch had exemplary faith" (17–18). O'Connor's Enoch is just the opposite. Whitt notes: "The name choice is a reminder that the faithful, trusting biblical Enoch never did go to hell; but this Enoch, who sells out to the modern materialistic world, will do just that. As an emery board is a rough surface for smoothing fingernails, Emery's personality irritates and grates on others." Margaret Earley Whitt, *Understanding Flannery O'Connor* (Columbia, SC: University of South Carolina Press, 1997), 18. I would also add that the emery board image plays an even more philosophical role than the one Whitt suggests, in that it also symbolizes the devolution of man and the removal of meaning in the world.

182. O'Connor, *Wise Blood*, 38.
183. O'Connor, *Wise Blood*, 44.
184. O'Connor, *Wise Blood*, 80.
185. O'Connor, *Wise Blood*, 83.
186. O'Connor, *Wise Blood*, 84.
187. Guardini notes, "There are various ways in which the mind reveals itself. In Augustine it does so in a peculiar tugging from 'below' to 'above,' from the transitory to the eternal, from the deficiencies of fragmentary to the full perfection of the essential. His is an idealistic spirituality—in Plato's sense." Guardini, *Augustine*, 37–38. Enoch Emory surrenders to the tugging from below and devolves into what is essentially a beast.
188. Bieber Lake, *Incarnational Art*, 61.
189. O'Connor, *Wise Blood*, 177–78.
190. O'Connor, *Wise Blood*, 179.
191. O'Connor, *Wise Blood*, 181–82.
192. O'Connor, *Wise Blood*, 195.
193. O'Connor, *Wise Blood*, 195.
194. O'Connor, *Wise Blood*, 198-99.
195. We step out of chronological order only to keep our arguments focused.
196. O'Connor, *Wise Blood*, 141.
197. O'Connor, *Wise Blood*, 176.
198. According to Aquinas, a human being is a composite of both body and soul, as the soul is the principle of life in a living body. Therefore, according to Thomas, at death one's soul is separated from one's left body, so that the soulless body is no longer a human being, but simply a corpse.
199. O'Connor, *Wise Blood*, 187.
200. O'Connor, *Wise Blood*, 187–88.
201. Bieber Lake, *Incarnational Art*, 76–77.
202. Consider Rayber (*The Violent Bear It Away*), Sheppard ("The

Lame Shall Enter First"), Hulga ("Good Country People"), Asbury ("The Enduring Chill"), Julian ("Everything That Rises Must Converge"), Thomas ("The Comforts of Home"), Calhoun ("The Partridge Festival"), etc.

[203] O'Connor, *Wise Blood*, 37.

[204] Aristotle, *Metaphysics*, 980a21.

[205] O'Connor, *Wise Blood*, 117.

[206] O'Connor, *Wise Blood*, 120.

[207] God is not willing Hazel to sin, but God's permissive will does allow Hazel to act in such a way that he will clearly experience the weight of his sin and so return to God, not unlike the younger son in the parable of the Prodigal Son (Luke 15:11-32). It is similar to what those in twelve-step programs call "hitting rock bottom." O'Connor writes, "Sin is a great thing as long as it is recognized. It leads a good many people to God who wouldn't get there otherwise." PJ, 26.

[208] O'Connor, *Wise Blood*, 127.

[209] O'Connor, *Wise Blood*, 67.

[210] O'Connor, *Wise Blood*, 126.

[211] O'Connor, *Wise Blood*, 113.

[212] O'Connor, *Wise Blood*, 112.

[213] O'Connor, *Wise Blood*, 204–05.

[214] O'Connor, *Wise Blood*, 207.

[215] O'Connor, *Wise Blood*, 208–09.

[216] O'Connor, *Wise Blood*, 210.

[217] There are scholars who reject this interpretation of Hazel's blinding. For instance, Susan Srigley argues, "With his blinding, Hazel isolates himself from all community; it is an intrinsic effect of the absolute freedom he preaches. He is separated from others and unable to love because of his belief in absolute spiritual and physical human independence from God and other human beings. Hazel Motes espouses a kind of penance that, instead of opening him to humility and to an awareness of human dependence, only reinforces his belief that responsibility can be

measured by the calculation of debts." Susan Srigley, *Flannery O'Connor's Sacramental Art* (Notre Dame: University of Notre Dame Press, 2004), 1–2. I find this interpretation interesting, but think it misunderstands the nature of the contemplative life, particularly in regard to community.

[218] "He might as well be one of them monks, she thought, he might as well be in a monkery." O'Connor, *Wise Blood*, 218.

[219] Haze literally throws his money away into a waste basket. O'Connor, *Wise Blood*, 220

[220] Although she would like to marry him, Haze has no interest in Mrs. Flood or in romantic relationships with any women, for his sole focus is his relationship with God. (O'Connor, *Wise Blood*, 223).

[221] He is obedient to a life of fasting, mortification, and penance, going so far as to put rocks in his shoes and wear barbed-wire strands around his chest and under his shirt. O'Connor, *Wise Blood*, 222, 224.

[222] In Hazel's blindness Mrs. Flood sees only the (self-inflicted) "breakdown of an apparatus," cf. Marcel in our discussion of "A Disregard for Mystery" above.

[223] Henry Edmondson, *Return to Good & Evil: Flannery O'Connor's Response to Nihilism* (New York: Lexington Books, 2002), 59.

[224] Guardini, *Spirit of the Liturgy*, 88–89.

[225] Cf. Edmondson, *Good & Evil*, 62–64.

[226] Edmondson, *Good & Evil*, 64.

[227] Bieber Lake, *Incarnational Art*, 89.

[228] Cf. Edmondson, *Good & Evil*, 65–70.

[229] O'Connor, *Wise Blood*, 232.

Acknowledgments

My warmest thanks to Joshua Hren for inviting me to publish this monograph with Wiseblood Books, to Mary Finnegan for her fine editing of the manuscript, and to Chris Scalia for writing a most warm and gracious introduction. I extend my deepest gratitude to my dear brother in Christ, Danny O'Brien, who always makes sure that my writing is better than good. And to Our Lady, who always has my back, thank you for being my shelter from the storm.

About Father Damian Ference

Father Damian Ference is a priest of the Diocese of Cleveland where he serves as vicar for evangelization and professor of philosophy at Borromeo Seminary. He turned his doctoral dissertation from the Pontifical University of St. Thomas Aquinas into an award-winning book entitled, *Understanding the Hillbilly Thomist: The Philosophical Foundations of Flannery O'Connor's Narrative Art* (Word on Fire, 2023), with a forward by his director, Thomas Joseph White, OP. That work focused on three main branches of philosophy—metaphysics, epistemology, and ethics—and explored how O'Connor's fiction is best understood against the backdrop of Thomism.

About Christopher Scalia

Christopher J. Scalia is a senior fellow at the American Enterprise Institute and co-editor of *On Faith: Lessons from an American Believer* (Crown Forum, 2019).

WISEBLOOD ESSAYS IN CONTEMPORARY CULTURE

Wiseblood Essays in Contemporary Culture offer in-depth interpretations of literature and art at large from a distinctly Catholic vantage point, while also championing and criticizing notable Catholic contributions to culture.

SELECTED TITLES

The Wayward Thomist:
A Critical Introduction to John Martin Finlay
James Matthew Wilson

A Theology of Fiction
Cassandra Nelson

Jane Austen's Darkness
Julia Yost

The Catholic Writer Today
Dana Gioia

"Everything Came to Me at Once":
The Intellectual Vision of René Girard
Cynthia L. Haven

How to Think Like a Poet
Ryan Wilson

Duty, the Soul of Beauty:
Henry James on the Beautiful Life
R. R. Reno

The Tragedy of the Republic
Pierre Manent

Death Comes for the Cathedrals
Marcel Proust

Poetry and Mysticism
Raïssa Maritain

T. S. Eliot: Culture and Anarchy
James Matthew Wilson

www.ingramcontent.com/pod-product-compliance
Lightning Source LLC
Chambersburg PA
CBHW070150080526
44586CB00015B/1929